Black Writers Redefine the Struggle
A TRIBUTE TO JAMES BALDWIN

Proceedings of a Conference
at the University of Massachusetts at Amherst
April 22-23, 1988

featuring
Chinua Achebe
Irma McClaurin-All
Andrew Salkey
Michael Thelwell
John Edgar Widema

D1569064

Edited by
Jules Chametzky

Published by
Institute for Advanced Study in the Humanities

Distributed by
University of Massachusetts Press

Copyright © 1989 by
The Institute for Advanced Study in the Humanities
Distributed by
The University of Massachusetts Press
Box 429
Amherst, Mass. 01004
All rights reserved
Printed in the United States of America
LC 88-29585
ISBN 0-87023-677-6

Library of Congress Cataloging-in-Publication Data

Black writers redefine the struggle.
   1. Baldwin, James, 1924-   —Criticism and
interpretation—Congresses.   2. Literature, Modern—
Black authors—History and criticism—Congresses.
3. Blacks—Intellectual life—Congresses.   I. Baldwin,
James, 1924-   II. Achebe, Chinua.   III. Chametzky,
Jules.   IV. University of Massachusetts at Amherst.
PS3503.A5527Z57   1989   818'.5409   88-29585
ISBN 0-87023-677-6

British Library Cataloguing in Publication data are available.

To James Arthur Baldwin
1924 - 1987

TABLE OF CONTENTS

PREFACE

JAMES BALDWIN began his formal academic connection with the five-college community (Amherst, Hampshire, Mount Holyoke, Smith Colleges, and the University of Massachusetts) as a Five College Professor of Literature in 1983-84, teaching at Hampshire, Smith, and the University. This appointment was to last three years; thereafter he became a member of the W.E.B. DuBois Department of Afro-American Studies and a Distinguished Fellow at the Institute for Advanced Study in the Humanities at the University of Massachusetts. He was highly satisfied with the latter arrangement. In addition to his pleasure in his colleagues and students his schedule allowed him to spend half his time at his home in France.

Chinua Achebe taught at the University of Massachusetts in the English and Afro-American Studies Departments from 1972-1974, shortly after the Biafran War. After another year of teaching at the University of Connecticut he returned to Nigeria as a Professor of Literature at his old university at Nsukka in 1976, where he remained until his retirement in 1983. He has since taught at U.C.L.A. and in Canada, and enjoys Emeritus status at Nsukka. He was awarded a Fulbright Professorship at the University of Massachusetts for the 1987-88 academic year, at the invitation of the Afro-American Studies Department and the Institute for Advanced Study in the Humanities.

Understandably, the prospect of these two outstanding writers and major cultural figures teaching in the same place, in the same year—at our University, in fact—engendered considerable excitement, especially among those concerned centrally with black life and culture in our time. A group of five-college faculty members involved with black literary studies began to meet at the Institute to plan a conference in the Spring of 1988 that would revolve around Achebe and Baldwin: one the prototypical writer of Africa—indeed, it would not be hyperbole to call him the father of modern African literature—the other the preeminent living embodiment of the literature of the Black Diaspora.

We determined at once that the occasion was not to be merely celebratory. It was to be a conference that would assess seriously where black writing, and beyond that the black struggle for full articulation, liberation, and recognition stood at this time and what its prospects and priorities might be. After much discussion, we agreed that the conference was to be called, challengingly we hoped, "Black Writers Redefine the Struggle."

Then the shock of Baldwin's death. After our initial numbness and grief, we decided to go ahead with the Conference, retitling it as a tribute to James Baldwin and focussing upon his impact on Black writing. We decided, further, instead of going far afield, to feature those writers who were in residence, as it were, among us and who had known and loved the man and his work. To our great pleasure, although it should not have surprised us, I suppose, considering the calibre of the contributors, the resulting conference was not just solemn memorial—it proved to be alive with wit, insight, variety, power and beauty. Or so it seemed to me. What follows are the proceedings of the conference held on April 22-23, 1988 at the University of Massachusetts/Amherst, from Chinua Achebe's provocative and wise opening night talk, through the next day's extraordinary readings in several genres and voices by Chinua Achebe, Irma McClaurin-Allen, Andrew Salkey, Michael Thelwell, John Wideman, ably and graciously introduced by Ketu Katrak, to the concluding collaborative, jazz-like panel discussion chaired by Esther Terry. Let the reader judge and, I hope, be touched and changed by it.

—*Jules Chametzky*
Director
Institute for Advanced Study in the Humanities

ACKNOWLEDGMENTS

I WANT TO THANK some of the people and organizations who made this occasion possible: Chancellor Joseph Duffey, Provost Richard O'Brien, Dean Murray Schwartz who made it possible to bring Chinua Achebe to the University of Massachusetts as a Fulbright Professor; the Black Studies Department of Amherst College and Rhonda Cobham-Sanders particularly; Reinhard Sanders of Hampshire College; Conn Nugent, Director of Five Colleges, Inc.; and the members of the Committee at the University—Joseph Skerrett, Ketu Katrak and John Wideman of the English Department; Mike Thelwell and Esther Terry of the Afro-American Studies Department, who were very significant in organizing and planning the conference. We are grateful to the authors and publishers of the poems read by Andrew Salkey for permission to reprint.—*J.C.*

ADDRESS

INTRODUCTION

MICHAEL THELWELL

AT THE INITIAL STAGES, well before this conference was even planned, when it became clear that Chinua was coming back from Nigeria to be here in the Valley, I remember many an evening myself and James Baldwin talking about it in a kind of gleeful excitement: next year, Chinua will be here. He could be sitting right here with us and there are so many things we could talk about. Well, before that could happen, the ancient drums beat and Jimmy danced and went to join the ancestors. And I remember before that happened, I'd sometimes see John, John Wideman, around town and John, as you know, is a very, very distinguished, able, and committed Afro-American novelist. And we'd pass the time of day, but before we left, some one of us would say, "Man, next year, next year, Jimmy and Chinua will be here." And we'd just start to grin at each other because we knew the exact sense in which all Black writers of a certain intention coming afterwards are profoundly and irrevocably in the debt of these two figures. They're the two defining presences of Black literature, in my mind, anyway, of Black writing in our time.

And despite the pretensions, the affectations of different other schools of thought and different other communities, I persist in the belief that history and politics and literature are inextricably intertwined. In this country, coming out of the 50s into the 60s at a time of a movement for Black liberation, when it became clear that all of America's assumptions would have to be redefined—that the nature of discourse on the question of the Black presence and its meaning would have to change forever—the history of that struggle threw up a presence, Jimmy Baldwin, which was the defining voice. He defined the way the terms of that debate would change and, in fact, the way serious Black writers write today. The way people who discuss the question of American reality and the question of the Black presence do so in terms that we inherited from, that were created by, that were projected by, the incredibly eloquent voice of Baldwin. And at the same time we were

2

affected by another motion, the motion of African independence, the force and tide of history, again. And out of that tumult and conflict, out came a voice standing astride it, defining it, translating African sensibilities, African realities and the density and complexity of African culture and reality into the flexible language, the English language in service to African realities— creating as he did so in many ways the modern African novel. And that was Chinua's voice. And between those two twin pillars, the rest of us who struggle and strive have illumining presences. Our work is enhanced but our challenge made more difficult by their example and presence. And looked at in that context, it's easy to understand why it didn't happen, why this town and this community were not slated to be distinguished by being able to say, for one year we had among us at the same time Chinua and Jimmy.

I just want your indulgence to briefly read a slight historical note on our speaker tonight. Sometime late in 1957, a package from Nigeria arrived unannounced in the offices of a London publisher. Its arrival occasioned some little uncertainty, no one at William Heineman and Co. having seen, or as I would hazard, ever having contemplated the possibility of, an African novel before. True, Nigeria and all of "British Africa" in the throes of pre-independence ferment were much in the British press. But an African novel? Finally, someone at the company remembered a lecturer at the London School of Economics who was recently returned from a tour of duty at the newly established University of Ghana, which is not quite Nigeria, but . . . not Nigeria, but at least next door. True, Professor Donald McCrae was a sociologist, but having at least seen West Africa, he was, one presumed, better than nothing. Infinitely better, it turns out. Not only could the sociologist read, but his now legendary report to the publisher was a model of pith, that economy for which the Scots are famed. What Professor McCrae wrote was one sentence: "The best first novel since the war." Finish. Kabisa.

That manuscript, since its publication as *Things Fall Apart* in 1958 on the eve of Nigerian independence, has sold three million copies in English. It has been translated into forty-five languages on every continent and is central to the curriculum of every African school system and most in the Caribbean. It was followed in 1960, the year of Nigerian independence, by *No Longer at Ease*, one million in English; in 1964 by the composite grandeur of the monumental *Arrow of God*, which was the first winner of the *New Statesman* award; and in 1967 by the wryly ironic and prophetic *Man of the People*, one of Anthony Burgess's ninety-nine best novels in English since the war; and this year there is *Anthills of the Savannah*, whose career is just launched. Thus far, it made the short list for Britain's Booker Prize, but the judges clearly lacked Professor McCrae's acumen. Doubly a shame, since the London bookmakers, who will bet on anything, had set it off at very very attractive odds, indeed. Aye, for a moment I thought my fortune was made.

3

On the surface, each of these highly acclaimed, beautifully achieved works do not really resemble their siblings. As Nerudin Farah, the Somalian novelist points out, *Anthills* is as different a novel as each of Achebe's has been from the one preceding it, or from the others that have come after. Which is quite true. All the works are different, very different. But what they all share in common is something in the genes of their paternity, the inheritance. Each reflects Mr. Achebe's uncanny instincts for those definitive illumining moments where past and future flash together in brief and telling conjunction, which have been called "those bloody intersections where history and literature meet." Each also proudly displays a fresh, deceptive, simple elegance of language, English to be sure, but a subtle English molded and fitted to the poetic necessities, the cultural resonances, and sensibilities of an African language and experience. Each also by a pervading aura of *gravitas*, the clear seriousness of the author's concerns and a sense that the writing and reading of novels is integral and necessary to the difficult process of the evolution of national consciousness and nation building. A seriousness in turn leavened by a controlled playfulness of spirit, an unerring eye for the absurd, and a gentle appreciation of the sharp ironies of post-colonial life. And finally, they are united by a quality of courage and candor, as expressed almost casually by the writer some twenty-five years ago: "Telling the truth is the only way, in the long run, you get listened to." And the world has listened to him, as you will do now. Thank you.

"SPELLING OUR PROPER NAME"

CHINUA ACHEBE

I'D LIKE TO BEGIN by thanking the Institute, Jules, for making this occasion possible. It's true that it has been marred by the death of James Baldwin, still it has been a very fruitful year for me and I appreciate all the help and all the attention that my family and I have received from the Institute and from the University. I have called my address "Spelling Our Proper Name."

In the April, 1988 number of *The World and I,* a *Washington Times* publication, there is a set of articles assembled in memory of James Baldwin. There were excerpts from *The Fire Next Time* and three commentaries, including a wise, sensitive appreciation by our own Bernard Bell.

The second commentator, a Mr. J.A. Parker, took quite a different light. He charged James Baldwin with failure to recognize "the widespread opportunities for advancement that existed in America and which were expanded as a result of the civil rights movement and white America's realization that segregation and racial discrimination were immoral." Instead of recognizing those facts, says Mr. Parker, Baldwin succumbed to hatred and rage which consumed both himself and his art.

The irritation in Mr. Parker's voice is unmistakable. One has heard it elsewhere. What does Baldwin want? Look, he has got a bunch of Black males controlling major U.S. cities, he's even got a few Black generals in the U.S. Army, and a whole lot of other gains. What does the fellow want?

The misunderstanding between such a view of the situation and James Baldwin's cannot but be fundamental. Baldwin wants something other than mayors and generals. He defines the struggle differently.

He wants to lift from the back of Black people the heavy burden of their blackness, to end the oppression which is visited on them because they are Black and for no other reason, to use his own phrase.

To define the struggle the way he does, Baldwin has to see it from a whole range of perspectives at once—the historical, the psychological, the philosophical, which are not present in a handful of statistics of recent advances. He has had to ask himself how long this struggle has gone on, what strategies have been used and to what effect, what gains have been made, yes, that too, but also what losses. But perhaps most important of all, Baldwin has had to wrestle to unmask the face of the oppressor and, seeing him clearly, call him by his proper name.

Listen to him: "I said that it was intended that you should perish in the ghetto. Perish by never being allowed to go behind the white man's definitions, by being never allowed to spell your name, your proper name." That was a letter to his nephew. A tightly compressed image of the ghetto here as both a physical urban location and a metaphysical zone of the mind, bounded and policed by the language of tinted, selective information. Hear him again: "Negroes want to be treated like men." In view of the advances made in unmasking the innate sexism of the English language, I will take the liberty to alter Baldwin's "men" to "people," although "people" lacks the archaic resonance of "men." But that's a price we should gladly pay in the interest of freedom and justice. Let me pursue this digression a little further and tell you if you don't know it already that this problem of saying "man" when you mean both "man" and "woman" does not exist in every language. In my native Igbo tongue, "man" has never been allowed so casually to embrace "woman" as in English. But to return to Baldwin and to the question what do Negroes want, "Negroes want to be treated like people." A perfectly straightforward statement containing seven words. People who have mastered Kant, Hegel, Shakespeare, Marx, Freud, and the Bible find this statement impenetrable. How can it be that such a simple demand, couched in language even a child can have no difficulty understanding, will defeat people who have understood the most abstruse thoughts and the world's great books. Surely this extraordinary failure to comprehend has to be something more than inability. It has to be a refusal, an act of will, a political strategy, a conspiracy.

Oppression does not automatically produce meaningful struggle. It has the ability to call into being a very wide range of responses between acceptance and violent rebellion. In between you can have a vague unfocused dissatisfaction. You can also have savage in-fighting among the oppressed, like the fierce love-hate entanglement with one another of crabs inside the fisherman's bucket, which has the result of ensuring that no crab gets away.

To answer oppression with appropriate resistance requires knowledge of two kinds. Self-knowledge by the victim means in the first place an awareness that oppression exists, that the victim has fallen from a great height of glory or promise into the present depths. Secondly, the victim must know who the enemy is. He must know his oppressor's *real* name, not an alias, not a pseudonym, not a *nom de plume.*

"Your name, sir. Please spell it!" Not very polite, perhaps; not very delicate. But Igbo people remind us that politeness is not enough to make a man swallow his phlegm for the sake of decorum. Baldwin understood and applied the wisdom of that proverb.

To demonstrate the importance of knowing the real name of the enemy, let me remind us of two stories made by our distant ancestors.

You remember that episode in the *Odyssey* where Odysseus tricks the Cyclops, Polyphemus, into calling him "no man" and how that mistake costs Polyphemus the help of his neighbors when he raises "a great and terrible cry." Of course, we're not expected to shed tears for Polyphemus for he is a horrible disgusting cannibal. Nevertheless, the story makes the point that in any contest, an adversary who fails to call his opponent by his proper name puts himself at risk.

From Homer and the Greeks to the Igbo of Nigeria. There is a remarkable little story which I took the liberty of adapting to my use in *Things Fall Apart,* which is the story of Tortoise and the Birds. I will summarize it here for those who are not familiar with that novel. The birds have been invited to a great feast in the sky and Tortoise is pleading with them to take him along. At first they are skeptical because they know how unreliable he is, but Tortoise convinces them that he's now a changed man, a born-again Tortoise, no less. So they agree and make him a pair of wings by donating one feather each. Not only that, they now fall for Tortoise's story that it is customary on such an important outing for people to take new praise names. The birds think this rather a charming idea and adopt it. They all take fanciful boastful titles, like Master of the Sky, Queen of the Earth, Streak of Lightning, Daughter of the Rainbow, and so on. The Tortoise announces his own choice. He is to be called All of You. The birds shriek with laughter and congratulate themselves on having such a funny fellow on their trip.

They arrive in the Sky and the Sky people set their great feast before them. Tortoise jumps up and asks, "Who is this feast intended for?" "All of you, of course," reply the hosts.

The birds do take their revenge by taking back their feathers and leaving Tortoise high and dry in the Sky, but that did not assuage their hunger as they flew all the way back to Earth on empty stomachs.

So the message is clear: we must not let our adversary, real or potential, assume a false name, even in playfulness.

Baldwin, belongs to mankind's ancient tradition of storytelling, to the tradition of prophets who had the dual role to *fore*-tell and to *forth*-tell. "If you know whence you came, there is really no limit to where you can go," he tells his nephew. An Igbo elder might have said exactly the same thing to the youngster. "If you can't tell where the rain began to beat you, you will not know where the sun dried your body." Literal minded, one-track mind people are exasperated by the language of prophets. Baldwin says to his nephew, "You come from a long line of great poets, some of the greatest poets since Homer. One of them said, 'The very time I thought I was lost, my dungeon shook and my chains fell off.'"

A bitter critic of Baldwin, one Stanley Crouch, writing in the *Village Voice*, dismisses such simplifications, that convinced Black nationalist automatons that they were the descendants of kings and queens brought in slave ships and should therefore uncritically identify with Africa. Baldwin would never advocate uncritical identification with anything. His mind was too sharp for that. Like a genuine artist, he always insisted that people should weigh things themselves and come to their own judgment. "Take no-one's word for anything, including mine," he says to his nephew. "But trust your experience." All the same, he felt deeply, instinctively, most powerfully, this need for the African American to know whence he came before he can know where he is headed.

The simple answer would be he came from Africa, of course. Not for Baldwin, however, any simple answers. Too much intelligence, too much integrity, for that. *What is Africa to me* asked an African poet who never left the motherland. Imagine then the tumult of questions in the mind of a man like Baldwin after three hundred traumatic years of absence. So in his anguished tribute to Richard Wright, he speaks of *the Negro problem and the fearful conundrum of Africa*. Fearful conundrum, terrifying problem admitting of no satisfactory solution.

I am not an Afro-American. It would be impertinent of me to attempt therefore to unravel this conundrum. But let me suggest two strands in this hideously tangled tissue of threads. One, the Africans sold us for cheap trinkets. Two, Africans have made nothing of which we can be proud.

I am not sure whether or not Baldwin referred specifically to the first question in his writings, but the second seriously troubled him and evoked the famous statement in "Stranger in the Village" in which he contrasts his heritage with that of a Swiss peasant. "The most illiterate among them is related in a way I am not to Dante, Shakespeare, Michelangelo, Aeschylus, Da Vinci, Rembrandt, and Racine. The cathedral at Chartres says something to them which it cannot say to me, as indeed would New York's Empire State Building should anyone here ever see it. Out of their hymns and dances come Beethoven and Bach. Go back a few centuries and they are in full glory—but I am in Africa, watching the conquerors arrive."

This lament issues not only from the heart of Black America, but also of Africa itself. The cure which literature can bring to human anguish of this magnitude is to prove its truth and history and so make it familiar and possible to live with. Unfortunately, the truth, the history about Black people has been so deeply buried in mischief and prejudice that a whole army of archeologists would now be needed to dig it out.

Before I go further, let me say two things. First, I do not see that it is necessary for any people to prove to another that they build cathedrals or pyramids before they can be entitled to peace and safety. Flowing from that, I do not believe that Black people should invent a great fictitious past in order to justify their human existence and dignity today. Baldwin is right when he says, "For the sake of one's children, in order to minimize the bill they must pay, one must be careful not to take refuge in any delusion." As it turns out, the telling of the story of Black people in our time and for a considerable period before, has been the self-appointed responsibility of white people and they have mostly done it to suit a white purpose.

Let us look at fairly recent events from African history. About A.D. 1600, a Dutch traveler to Benin, modern Nigeria, had no difficulty in comparing the city of Benin most favorably with Amsterdam. The main street of Benin, he tells us, was seven or eight times wider than its equivalent, the Warmoes in Amsterdam. The houses were in as good a state as the houses in Amsterdam.

Two hundred years later, before the British sacked the city of Benin, they first called it "The City of Blood" whose barbarism so revolted the British conscience that they dispatched a huge army to overwhelm it, banish its king, and loot its royal art gallery for the benefit of the British Museum and numerous private collections. All this was done, it was said with the straightest of faces, to end repugnant practices like human sacrifice. But the real reason was the fact that the British wanted to remove an obstacle to the penetration of the rich palm and rubber hinterland by British commercial, political, and religious groups.

Those who speak so feelingly about the progress made by Black people in one place or another may wish to hear the story of the most remarkable progress by Black Africans in West Africa during the second half of the 19th century.

The attempt by the British to occupy West Africa physically in the first half of the century was a total disaster. In the year 1859 alone, one-half of the entire European population of Freetown perished from tropical diseases. That was the West Africa that earned the dubious title of "The White Man's Grave." A lugubrious and anonymous English poet exclaimed these lines of lament to the terrible coast of West Africa of those days: "Bight of Benin, Bight of Benin/Where few come out, though many go in."

Oppression, which is only one species of power use, has as much need of intelligence and sophistication as any other if it is to survive. It cannot do so on mere bullishness. So the British colonial experiment, faced with extinc-

9

tion in the hostile West African environment, wrote up new high-minded policies to meet the emergency. Henceforth, it proclaimed, the Africans themselves and people of African descent must bear the burden of the civilizing mission among their own people. The "progress" made under this new policy included the incredible fact that a Black man was actually appointed governor of Freetown in the 1850s. This period also saw the consecration of a Yoruba ex-slave, Adjayi Crowther, at St. Paul's Cathedral in London in 1864 as Bishop of the sprawling diocese of West Equatorial Africa. It also saw the recruitment of Caribbean Blacks as missionaries and artisans in West Africa. Meanwhile, the British, believing like one of their songs that you should pray to God but keep your powder dry, intensified their search for the enemy, malaria. The search was soon rewarded when an English medical scientist, Dr. Ross, working in India, tracked the scourge of malaria to the mosquito. In a few years, the situation changed. Malaria could now be controlled. West Africa ceased to be The White Man's Grave, and all of a sudden the need for the high-minded policies of Africanization no longer existed. You would think that the old policy might be slowly and gracefully changed. But no! The old Bishop Crowder was literally hounded out of his episcopal see and replaced by a white bishop. Africans in high places in government or commerce were removed or superceded. The West Indians were sent packing. Things stayed that way for the next three quarters of a century, until independence came to British West African colonies in the wake of the general collapse of the British Empire at the end of the second world war.

The anti-Black period in modern colonial West African history was accompanied by a virulently racist literature. The frankness of those days was nowhere better demonstrated than in an editorial in *The Times* of London when Durham University agreed to affiliate with Fourab College in Freetown, Sierra Leone. *The Times* asked Durham quite pointedly if it might consider affiliating to the zoo!

Apart from the vast quantity of offensive and trashy writing about Africa in Victorian England and later, a more serious colonial genre, as John Meyers calls it, also developed at this time, beginning with Kipling in the 1880s, proceeding through Conrad to its apogee in E.M. Forster, and down again to Joyce Cary and Graham Greene.

John Buchen was in the middle ground between the vulgar and the serious. He was also interesting for combining a very senior career in colonial administration with novel writing. What he says about natives in his novels takes on therefore the additional significance of coming out of the horse's mouth. Here is what an approved character in one of his novels, *Prester John* says: "That is the difference between White and Black, the gift of responsibility. As long as we know and practice it, we will rule not in Africa alone, but wherever there are dark men who live only for their bellies." White racism, then, is a matter of politics and also economics. The history and the truth of the black man, told by the white man, has generally been done to serve political and economic ends.

Baldwin says, "Take no-one's word for anything, including mine.... Know whence you came. If you know whence you came, there is really no limit to where you can go. The details and symbols of your life have been deliberately constructed to make you believe what White people say about you.... It was intended that you should perish in the ghetto, perish by . . . never being allowed to spell your proper name."

Let us now look briefly at the "fearful conundrum" of Africans selling their brothers and sisters and children for a bauble. Was that truly what happened? Has anyone told us the sad, sad story of that King of Bukongo who reigned as a Christian king, having changed his name to Dom Alfonso I, from 1506 to 1543? Dom Alfonso, who built schools and churches and renamed his capital San Salvador, whose son was bishop of Utica in Tunisia and from 1521 bishop of the Congo, who sent embassies to Lisbon and to Rome. This man thought he had allies and friends in the Portuguese Jesuits he had encouraged to come and live in his kingdom and convert his subjects. Unfortunately for him, Brazil was opening up and needing labor to work the vast plantations. So the Portuguese missionaries switched professions. They abandoned their preaching and became slave raiders. Dom Alfonso, in bewilderment, wrote letters in 1526 to King John III of Portugal complaining about the behavior of his subjects in the Congo. The letter was unanswered. In the end, the Portuguese succeeded in arming rebellious chiefs to wage war on the king. They defeated him. Thereafter, the Portuguese imposed the payment of tribute in slaves on the kingdom.

You will not find this story in our conventional history books. So for a start, we must change our reading lists. Such books as Chancellor Williams' *Destruction of Black Civilization;* Chinweizu's *The West and the Rest of Us;* and especially Cheik Anta Diop's *The African Origin of Civilization* should be standard fare for us and our children.

These are not fanciful books. In 1966, at the First World Festival of Black and African Arts held in Dakar, Dr. Diop, who had then been working for twenty years on rediscovering African history, shared with W.E.B. Dubois an award as the writer who had exerted the greatest influence on Negro thought in the 20th century. Dr. Diop, an African Renaissance man— physicist, historian, poet—was until his death recently Director of the Radiocarbon Laboratory at the University of Dakar. His revolutionary work, enormous in scope and quality and pursued with zeal and intelligence over a period of forty years, has given Black people a foundation on which to begin a reconstruction of their history.

11

Who created the world's first and longest lasting civilization on the banks of the Nile? White people, of course. Wrong. Black people, who, as if they knew what was coming, had called their country Kemit, which means "black," long before the Greeks called it Egypt.

But even that ancient precaution was not going to be enough. European scholars and encyclopedia tell us that ancient Egypt was called Kemit because the soil of the Nile valley was black! I suppose they took the analogy of White Russia, which was presumably so named because of the snow on the ground! We won't go into this now, but I strongly recommend Cheik Anta Diop's books as we redefine our struggle. If you did no more than look at the photographs of the Negro faces of the early pharaohs, the first Pharaoh, Menes the Ethiopian prince who united Upper and Lower Egypt, his face like the face of a Nigerian chief, or the clear Bantu profile of the great Sphinx as the French scientific expedition saw it in the last century; or the god Osiris with his clear Negro features—if you saw only that, you would have started something which is guaranteed to grow on you, the reclaiming of our history.

Good writers have a good nose for this kind of thing. I was not surprised therefore to see in John Wideman's last novel, *Reuben*, the beginnings of an adventure with Egypt; or Alice Walker dispatching one-half of the story of *The Color Purple* to Africa; or Toni Morrison and a host of other novelists and poets probing with increasing assurance "the fearful conundrum of Africa." Thank you. □

READINGS

CHINUA ACHEBE

POEMS

It's a great pleasure to welcome all of you this morning and also to welcome all our writers, to thank them for their participation in this conference, which is entitled "Black Writers Redefine the Struggle: A Tribute to James Baldwin." As was remarked yesterday, when we all started planning this conference last year, there was a great sense of excitement at the prospect of having two writers of the significance of Chinua Achebe and James Baldwin in our midst at the same time. And very sadly indeed for all of us, Baldwin is no longer with us today. However, we all collectively wish to remember and to acknowledge the many monumental contributions to the struggle of Black people wherever they may reside that Baldwin has made. Baldwin's beautiful words which were quoted yesterday by Achebe may be, I thought, an appropriate place to begin this morning. Baldwin, in a letter to his nephew, had remarked, and I'm paraphrasing, as long as you know where you're coming from, you can go anywhere. That is the spirit in which Black writers carry the responsibility of redefining the struggle, a spirit that is serious, self-assured, and dedicated to the people and to their various communities. Our writers will read from their work and they will read in the order that appears in the program, which is alphabetically arranged, so we will begin with Chinua Achebe and move on to the end to John Wideman.

It has indeed been a great treat to have Chinua Achebe here with us at the University this academic year as a Fulbright professor. I personally can say that I have learned a great deal from him by simply listening to him and have marveled at his great skill in telling stories, at his wisdom, which is often cloaked in the most deceptively simple and lucid expressions, at his manner, which is always gentle, even humble, and also at his lively wit and sense of humor. The author of such remarkable achievements as Things Fall Apart, Arrow of God, and most recently, his novel Anthills of the Savannah, Achebe is also the author of children's stories, poems, and essays. It is a great pleasure to welcome Chinua Achebe.

—Ketu Katrak

I DIDN'T LOOK at the program properly; I had the impression that I was coming towards the end. This alphabetical thing. . . . OK, those of you who were here last night probably noticed that I was having difficulty with my voice. It has not improved, if anything, maybe it's a bit worse, so I'm going to limit myself to perhaps two passages. I want to take the first passage from my new novel, *Anthills of the Savannah.* I was thinking of something that would be somehow appropriate to the occasion, especially to the memory of James Baldwin, and so I decided to read "The Hymn to the Sun." This is a poem written by one of the characters in the novel, Ikem, and it's, as the title says, it is a hymn to the sun. The sun in my mythology is very close to the Almighty. The sun is the eye of Chuku. Chuku has one eye which looks at the world, and that's the sun. The sun is also seen as a carrier of sacrifice to Chuku. The supreme god is so powerful to you, that he doesn't play any significant role in the day to day life of the people. He's too important for that. But there's only one occasion in Igbo religion when a sacrifice is made to Chuku, and that's the last, when everything else fails. Then a sacrifice might be given to him and it is the sun who carries this sacrifice. This poem reflects the problem, one of the key problems, in this story, in this novel. And one of the key problems of Africa today, the drought. Ikem has written this poem, perhaps a day or two before his flat was searched and he was taken away and he never came back. This poem was picked off the floor by his friend, and the other character, Chris.

"THE HYMN TO THE SUN:"

Great Carrier of Sacrifice to the Almighty, Single Eye of God! Why have you brought this on us? What hideous abomination, forbidden and forbidden and forbidden again seven times, have we committed or else condoned? What error that no reparation can hope to erase?

Look, our forlorn prayers, our offerings of conciliation lie scattered about your floor where you cast them disdainfully away; and every dawn you pile up your long basket of day with the tools and emblems of death.

Wide-eyed, insomniac, you go out at cock-crow, spitting malediction at a beaten recumbent world. Your crimson torches fire the furnaces of Heaven and the roaring holocaust of your vengeance fills the skies.

Undying Eye of God! You will not relent, we know it, from compassion for us. Relent then for your own sake; for that bulging eye of madness that may be blinded by soaring motes of an incinerated world. Single Eye of God, will you put yourself out merely that man may stumble in your darkness? Remember, Single Eye, one-wall-neighbor-to-Blindness, remember!

What has man become to you, Eye of God, that you should hurt yourself on his account? Has he grown to such god-like stature in your sight? Homeward-bound from your great hunt, the carcass of an elephant on your great head, do you now dally on the way to pick up a grasshopper between your toes?

Great Messenger of the Creator! Take care that the ashes of the world rising daily from this lyre may not prove enough when they descend again to silt up the canals of birth in the season of renewal.

The birds that sang the morning in had melted away even before the last butterfly fell roasted to the ground. And when song birds disappeared, morning herself went into the seclusion of a widow's penance in soot and ashes, her ornaments and fineries taken from her—velvets of soft elusive light and necklaces of pure sound lying coil upon coil down to her resplendent breasts: corals and blue chalcedonies, jaspers and agates veined like rainbows. So the songbirds left no void, no empty hour when they fled, because the hour itself had died before them. Morning no longer existed.

The trees had become hydra-headed bronze statues so ancient that only blunt residual features remained on the faces, like anthills surviving to tell the new grass of the savannah about last year's brush fires.

Household animals were all dead. First the pigs, fried in their own fat; and then the sheep and goats and cattle, choked by their swollen tongues. Stray dogs in the market-place in a running battle with vultures devoured the corpse of the madman they found at last coiled up one morning in the stall over which he had assumed unbroken tenancy and from where he had sallied forth every morning to mount the highest rung of the log steps at the center of the square and taunt the absent villagers. Where is everybody? You have not forgotten your own market day? Come! Bring your long baskets of yams and your round baskets of cocoyams. Where are the fish women and the palm oil women, where the high head loads of pottery? Come, today may be your lucky day, the day you may find a blind man to trade against. You have nothing to sell? Who said so? Come! I will buy your mother's cunt.

The dogs growled as they tore him apart and snapped at the vultures who struck back fearlessly with their beaks. After that last noisy meal, the vultures pushed in their wicked bashed-in heads and departed for another country.

In the end, even the clouds were subdued though they had held out longest. Their bedraggled bands rushed their last pathetic resources from place to place in a brave but confused effort to halt the monumental formations of the Sun's incendiary hosts. For this affront, the Sun wreaked a terrible vengeance on them, cremating their remains to their last plumes and scattering the ashes to the four winds. Except that the winds had themselves fled long ago. So the clouds' desecrated motes hung so splendid in a mist across the whole face of the sky, and gave the Sun's light glancing off their back, the merciless tint of bronze. Their dishonored shades sometimes would stir in futile insurrection at the spirit-hour of noon, starting a sudden furious whirling of ash and dust, only to be quickly subdued again.

In last desperate acts, the Earth would now ignite herself and send up a shield of billowing black smoke over her head. It was pitiful and misguided, for the heat of the brushfires merely added to the fire of the Sun. And soon, anyhow, there was no fodder left to burn.

No one could say why the Great Carrier of Sacrifice to the Almighty was doing this to the world, except that it had happened before, long, long ago in legend. The earth broke the hoes of the gravediggers and bent the iron tip of their spears. Then the people knew the time had come to desert their land, abandoning their unburied dead and even the dying, compounding thereby whatever abominations had first unleashed the catastrophe. They travelled by starlight and lay under the shade of their mats by day until the sands became too hot to lie upon. Even legend is reticent about their plight, accounting only that every night when the journey began again, many failed to rise from under their mats and that those who did stagger up cast furtive glances at the silent shelters and set their stony faces to the south. And by way of comment the voice of legend adds that the man who deserts his town and shrine house, who turns his face resolutely away from a mat shelter in the wilderness where his mother lies and cannot rise again, or his wife or child, must carry death in his eyes. Such was the man and such his remnant fellows who one night set upon the sleeping inhabitants of the tiny village of Ose and wiped them out and drank the brown water in their wells and took their land and renamed it Abazan.

And now the times had come round again out of story-land. Perhaps not as bad as the first times, ye. But they could easily end worse. Why? Because today no one can rise and march south by starlight, abandoning crippled kindred in the wild savannah, and arrive stealthily at a tiny village and fall upon its inhabitants and slay them and take their land and say: I did it because death stared through my eye.

So they send instead a deputation of elders to the government who hold the yam today, and hold a knife, to seek help of them.

I will read one last poem, in Igbo. This poem is a dirge. It's a poem I wrote in 1967 or thereabouts when my friend the poet Christopher Okigbo, was killed in battle. The form is a traditional Igbo dirge, it's a hymn, the song that people sing when a member of their age-grade dies and the members of the age-set go around the village singing and the idea is that they don't believe that death has happened. They pretend that the member of their age-grade has only gone to the stream, or has gone to the forest to fetch firewood, or something like that. And it's only when they have gone around the entire village and the person is still missing that they then finally accept the death.

UNO-ONWU OKIGBO

Obu onye k'ayi nacho?
Obu onye k'ayi nacho?
Okigbo k'ayi Nacho
    Nzomalizo

Ojelu nku, nya nata!
Ochuli'iyi, nya nata!
Ojel'afia, nya nata!
Okigbo k'ayi nacho
    Nzomalizo

Obu onye k'ayi nacho?
Obu onye k'ayi nacho?
Okigbo k'ayi Nacho
    Nzomalizo

Ojebe nku, Ogboko elinia!
Ochube mmili, lyi elinia!
Ojebe afia, uzu-afia soolia!
Ojebe agha, Ogbonuke biko chaalia!
Okigbo k'ayi nacho
    Nzomalizo

Ezite egwu, onye gagbalayi?
Eseta ogu, onye gagbalayi?
Onye anakpo nwel'ife oneme!
Okigbo k'ayi nakpo!
    Nzomalizo

Ngwa, nee egwu k'onabia!
Ifugo na agha awa?
Ogu egweu choo! Dike n'ogu chaa!!
Ifurozi na onye anakpo nwel' ife oneme!

A WAKE FOR OKIGBO

translated by I. Feanyi Menkiti and Chinua Achebe

For whom are we looking?
For whom are we looking?
For Okigbo we are looking.
    Nzomalizo!

Has he gone for firewood
    let him return!
Has he gone to fetch water
    let him return!
Has he gone to the marketplace
    let him return!
For Okigbo we are looking!
    Nzomalizo!

For whom are we looking?
For whom are we looking?
For Okigbo we are looking!
    Nzomalizo!

Has he gone for firewood
    may Ugboko not take him!
Has he gone to the stream
    may Iyi not swallow him!
Has he gone to the market, then keep from him
    you Tumult of the marketplace!
Has he gone to battle, please Ogbonuke
    step aside for him!
For Okigbo we are looking!
    Nzomalizo!

They bring home a dance, who is to dance it for us?
They bring home a war who will fight it for us?
The one we call repeatedly, there's something
    he alone can do
It's Okigbo we're calling!
    Nzomalizo!

21

Witness the dance how it arrives!
And the war how it has broken out!
But the caller of our dance is nowhere to be found
The brave one in battle is nowhere in sight!
Do you not see now that whom we call again
And again, there is something only he can do?
It is Okigbo we are calling!
>Nzomalizo!

The dance ends abruptly!
The spirit dancers fold their dance and depart in mid-day;
Rain soaks the stalwart, soaks the two-sided drum!
The flute is broken that elevates the spirit
The music pot shattered that accompanies the leg in its measure;
Brave one of my blood! Brave one of Igboland!
Brave one in the middle of so much blood!
Owner of riches in the hometown of spirits!
Okigbo is the one I am calling!
>Nzomalizo!

NOTES

1) *Nzomalizo*
   This refrain does not have a precise meaning. Its principal element is the word *zo* meaning *to hide*. The doubling of *zo* in association with the other sounds in the refrain introduce the notion of playfulness, as in hide-and-seek.

2) *Ugboko*
   The forest personified.

3) *Iyi*
   The stream personified.

4) *Ogbonuke*
   The maker of disasters. Literally Ogbonuke means the entirety of one's age-set. Symbolically it is the resentful anger of members of this set who have died pre maturely and violently.

IRMA McCLAURIN-ALLEN

PROSE AND POEMS

*From Africa, now to the United States. Our next writer is Irma McClaurin-Allen—
who is the author of two books of poetry,* Black Chicago *and* Song in the Night. *Her
poems have also appeared in a number of periodicals. She has received the Gwendolyn
Brooks Award for Poetry in 1975. Irma McClaurin-Allen is currently working on a
biography of the life of the Afro-American journalist Leanita McClain and the forthcoming biography is entitled* Incongruities: A Biography of Leanita McClain.
*Irma is a lecturer in Women's Studies at the University of Massachusetts and is the
Assistant Dean in the College of Arts and Sciences. She has a third volume of poems
which is forthcoming from Lotus Press and she'll be reading from that today. The
volume is entitled* Pearl's Song.

—*Ketu Katrak*

LET ME SAY that it is indeed an honor to share the podium with my brothers here, many of whom have served as inspiration to me as a writer. What I'd like to do is read briefly from *Incongruities: A Biography of Leanita McClain* and then move to the poetry. I'll begin by reading a brief section from the introduction:

> Leanita McClain was a black journalist who in 1984 committed suicide at the age of 32. She was a writer for the *Chicago Tribune* and she was the first black and the second woman to sit on the editorial board of the *Chicago Tribune*.
>
> No one will ever know the real reasons behind Leanita's decision to commit suicide. In my mind it was a confluence of many factors: racism, depression, alienation, failed personal relationships, value conflicts, eroding support systems, coupled with Leanita's fragile sensibility, her vulnerability as an intellectually astute, politically insightful, aspiring black female that configured in the development of a despair so acute and hopelessness so great that she felt life was not worth living. Some of us encounter the same circumstances and are able to move on. Leanita obviously could not and, no doubt, there are other reasons which will remain hidden because friends prefer to remain silent or because the incidents could not be documented. I have set myself the task to write Leanita's life history because of the elegance of her writings and the truths therein which she revealed so eloquently. And because other young, intelligent, aspiring women, regardless of race, may be travelling this same complex path. I have chosen to tell Leanita's story so that we may read and be forewarned, so that we may learn and cherish the simple axiom, "but for the grace of God, there go I."

This is from the first chapter:

> The first day of school for Leanita was probably a mixture of trepidation and excitement as she kissed her mother goodbye in the schoolyard. She would leave for a while the secure world she shared with her family inside the apartment of Ida B. Wells' projects. But she would also begin to experience for herself the attraction of learning, inspired by her sisters, those good students in high school. She had been trying to follow them to school since she was four.

The Doolittle School was located at 535 East 35th St., about five blocks from Leanita's home. It was "made up of two three-story buildings—one of gingerbread red brick built in the past century, and one of gray brick that dates from the early forties. The two buildings were connected by a passageway." The facility had a reputation for being the best Black elementary school on the south side. Some kids like Michael Jones, Leanita's childhood friend, found their parents had moved into the projects because of its educational advantages. Most of the reputation derived from teachers like Grace Simms Holt, who hailed from the Atlanta tradition. Graduates of Black institutions like Spelman and Morehouse, they were noted for their *hauteur* and could trace their intellectual lineage back to W.E.B. DuBois and the talented tenth. It was this arrogance and a profound belief in the ability of Blacks to achieve high intellectual standards that set Grace somewhat apart from some of her colleagues raised in the city. It is also what inspired her to approach her teaching and students with love, affection, and high expectations.

Doolittle was unusual in the educational environment that it was able to create for its students. This uniqueness was affirmed by the interest of the National College of Education in the school. By the time Leanita had entered the sixth grade, the NCE had proposed a project which would enhance the educational creativity already occurring in the classroom. An aspect of the project enabled Grace Simms Holt and other teachers to delve into the literature which began with an assumption that Blacks suffered from "negative self-images." They also attended classes on Saturdays as part of the ironically named "Value-Sharing Project." This willingness on the part of the teachers to go beyond the school requirements and take classes on Saturdays was indicative of the energy which permeated the school. They wanted to give more to their students. Grace Simms Holt had in fact requested that she be allowed to keep her class of highly talented young students for the next three years so that she could maintain the continuity in their learning process. Leanita was among the group. Though the project allowed discussion on a variety of subjects, Holt felt that it "seemed to want to show values of versimilitude, love, and affection which the families already had." The parents she encountered were like the McClains in their love and concern for their children, though they may have manifested them differently. They were tough, and put pressure on the children because they believed, as Grace did, that if one was black, one had to be better than one's white counterparts.

Rather than react to the nomenclature of the project, which assumed the negative self-image stereotype was true, Grace used it in her classroom to reveal to her students how they were perceived by the White world. The responses to the topic varied, but she found that for Leanita, "the whole idea of Black people being presented as a problem was a problem." Leanita was shocked to learn that she was supposed to be culturally deprived and it made her angry. As early as seventh and eighth grade she knew that the world always saw her through those eyes and she would have to disprove the myth, the image, the stereotypes.

Early on, Leanita seemed to strive to correct these faulty images against which her talents and those of other Black students were measured. The world she lived in was one in which people were "very concerned," there was a "strong sense of community and a great deal of support and encouragement from neighbors; parents involved themselves in the PTA" and so she was used to acknowledgement of her achievements. The Black families in Ida B. Wells were not like the "textbook nuclear families," but more a social structure of extended familial relationships, the forms of which dated back to slavery. Leanita and the other kids knew that "if they didn't do well," they had "disappointed more than their family." The lessons they learned in Miss Simms Holt's class were not always confined to analyzing sociological texts. They read newspapers, discussed problems in their community, and basically confronted the reality of the world in which they lived in order to examine their place in it. On one occasion a bus load of children went downtown as part of a fieldtrip to visit Carson Pierre Scott, a large department store where Blacks were beginning to spend increasing amounts of money. Grace Simms Holt had complete confidence in this group of eighth graders whom she had nurtured for two years already. They were accompanied by two parents who enjoyed these opportunities. Limited finances and a perception of the Loop as a white domain kept many of the children and their families from shopping or visiting downtown.

As the group waited for the bus, they discovered the drivers did not want to let such a large group on at one time. Although crowded buses were not unusual in Chicago, the sight of twenty Black schoolchildren and three Black adults taking a bus to the near-white downtown may have been the real reason for refusal. Eventually the group reached their destination, enthusiastic about visiting what was one of the Loop's better stores. But the event proved not a joyous one for Grace Simms Holt: "You would have thought I had brought a group of criminals into the store. They had guards and people following us around all over the store as we went through. I was never so insulted in all the days of my life." But just confronting racism was not the end of

27

the fieldtrip. Understanding it was vital. And so for Leanita and the rest of the class, the incident "turned into a theme that we wanted to investigate in terms of structural racism, the kinds of things that you encounter as a Black person and for them to know that when you encounter it, it's not you. There's nothing that you've done but the fact that you came in [as part of] a group and that you were [perceived by Whites] as someone who came into the store and had to be watched all the time, [this is what] was so insulting." It was a lesson that Leanita would recall years later.

This is a section from Leanita in high school and it begins with an epigraph from one of her poems. It's a kind of coda that repeats itself in some of her writing: "To be me is to be nothing/To be nothing is to be me."

On the verge of adolescence, Leanita enrolled in high school in September, 1965; she would reach her fourteenth birthday the next month. Leatrice, her sister, had married in July, 1961 and Anita followed three months later in October. And so Leanita lived her adolescent years as an only child.

Reaching Lucy Flower High School on the west side of Chicago meant rising in the near dark of fall and winter to catch the El train for a long ride. Leanita usually travelled with Dena Joy Hurst, a friend she had known since she was "three (or four, or something)." They'd grown up together, meeting when their parents sat in the park to talk. Dena and Leanita were an incongruous pair. Dena was tall, dark, and "terribly loud and outspoken." Though her mother was a strict and religious woman, Dena enjoyed shocking people by her use of vulgar language and would frighten Leanita at times by her familiarity with the winos and prostitutes who inhabited the streets between their homes and the subway station. What drew them together was Dena's honesty. Leanita wrote, "I also admire Dena because she will not talk about anyone behind their backs," and for the fact that she was "sweet and understanding."

Though very good friends, their personalities were the antithesis of each other. Years later, Leanita would refer to Dena as her "alter ego." "Dena and I are exact opposites. Dena is loud, outspoken, rough and ready, and me, I'm just me. Shy, timid, quiet little me!" Dena was a survivor and knew it was better to relinquish pleasantries and run innocuous errands than to offend. In treating the street inhabitants just like regular people, she acquired a kind of immunity to the harshness of street life; the winos and prostitutes treated her like a kid sister. No one bothered her or her friends or offered them drugs. Street people would protect her from the life they had come to know.

The subway took them through the bowels of the city, stopping at dimly lit stations that smelled of urine. Downtown at Van Buren and State, they left the subterranean station and emerged at ground level. In the early morning, few people got on and off at the popular stops of Jackson or Randolph in the Loop, where Whites seemed to dominate the world. Those who did were "dull, drab, and groggy," and most often Black, on their way to clean floors or straighten up storerooms before businesses opened. Here in the quiet of the early morning gray light, the stores did not seem so powerful and the windows were perhaps not so magical and tempting. Slowly Dina and Leanita climbed the long iron stairs upward to the elevated platform where they continued their journey. Occasionally a swift chill from the lake-front breeze invaded the El train as the doors opened and closed.

From this altitude they looked down upon life in Chicago. Going from the south side of Chicago to the west side meant seeing some changes occur in the landscape. From the tiny rowhouses of Ida B. Wells, they watched dwellings become brick duplexes, apartment buildings and houses, where clothes flapped on lines strung from windows in winter and summer. These were pockets after pockets of dismal high-rise projects huddled against the bareness of the sky. Forlorn, their darkened windows in the early morning did nothing to reveal the explosion of life which might awaken in a few hours.

After a two hour journey, the two girls finally arrived at their destination. Chicago's west side was not that different from Leanita's home turf. Churches dotted every corner, neighborhood stores were already throbbing with life to accommodate those people who had to get to work early but needed to shop for a few things first. Here lunchmeat was ten cents higher than what you paid at the big supermarkets and sometimes the vegetables were brown around the edges, but there was a conspiracy between the shoppers and the neighborhood store-keepers, a conspiracy of survival. People endured the higher prices because of the convenience and because of the familiarity they developed with a few of the store owners. Because of that familiarity, they sent their young children to fetch groceries when they were too sick or too tired to go out without fear of being cheated. They charged the food necessary for the family to survive that week and paid for it on Friday when their paycheck, welfare check, or unemployment check arrived. At the White stores, on the other hand, they were just another Black face and cash on the barrel was the only language understood. In the ghettoes (south and west sides) there was another language at work. Some of the shopkeepers lived in the neighborhood, others did not, but they shared in the triumphs and woes of the community, often using their stature as a businessman to get bail for someone's teenage son in jail or training one of the neighborhood girls as a cashier so she could find a job downtown.

At the end of their trip, Leanita and Dena left the dark iron labyrinth of the El station, journeying downward into the throbbing light they had merrily watched from their elevated windows. Even early in the morning, music sometimes blared out from a corner tavern and workmen milled around the factories, scattered up and down Lake Street eating their dinner or breakfast, depending on which shift they were on. Probably not until she reached the brown wooden doors of the school was Leanita comfortable. In the milieu of school she overcame her shyness to involve herself in learning and extracurricular activities.

Lucy Flower was a "four-story sand-colored building" located at 3545 West Fulton, one block from the Lake Street El tracks. It was "about a half-block square opposite the Garfield Park Conservatory," where on certain days Leanita and a group of her friends would take their lunches. Amid the humid floral jungle and solitude of the conservatory, it was possible to relax momentarily and forget the realities of the day.

On warm spring days, girls lounged outside on the steps of the school, giggling at or ignoring completely the cars of young Black men which cruised the area. They would fill the quiet morning air with their voices until the bell rang, going inside to continue their affair with books and typewriters. Occasionally a few might remain behind. Those who did would be propositioned by an older Black or White man driving around the area. Slowly the crowd of suave Black men would drift away, destined to return again at lunchtime. The ones who failed to leave might find themselves interrogated by the police, who appeared unexpectedly after a discreet call from the assistant principal or one of the teachers concerned about their girls.

I will now read a poem from my new book (*Pearl's Song*, Lotus Press, 1988) entitled "Home." I was reading Baldwin again this morning and he talks about how for a writer it's so critical to write from one's own experience. I went to high school with Leanita McClain and so a lot of what's in the biography is sort of my story as well.

HOME

I walk along forgotten streets
where parking lots cover places
that once held stores

I stole from.
Addiction Centers
overshadow taverns.
Forgotten people centers
(Black centers)
now act as salvation armies:
Old clothes
Old people
Old dreams . . .
if you want them.

I step over forgotten holes
in the streets
that have captured
many a victim
for thieves.
I shrink from hallways and alleys
that have witnessed too many
X-rated scenes
and wonder . . .
if I'll ever return.

And these last two I'd like to dedicate to the memory of James Baldwin.
This one is called "Moving to a Better Thang."

MOVING TO A BETTER THANG

I have come to know the map of your face
lines stretching across an ecru surface
crossroads always intersecting.

once you spoke of your life:
a forty year baptism.
others lost, drowned by a different current.

you spoke of revolutionary obituaries with reverence;
of prophets: poets stretched too tightly
across the frame of the american dream;
poets wounded by bullets from trigger-happy priests,
poets with dead visions riding merry-go-rounds of pain;
poets slitting their wrists, watching final blood verses
refusing to coagulate into something other than none
sense.

31

Because you spoke then
I know that when your eyes sparkle
(twin coals)
they are diamonds waiting to cut
through the hardcore shit of our disillusionment.

And this final poem was in fact written for Leanita. It's entitled "Eulogy for a Friend."

EULOGY FOR A FRIEND

Sweet nightingale
even now your song recedes
in the half-lit corridors of memory
where sad, troubled eyes peer out
from yearbook pages.

Once your quicksilver smile
spun light onto impenetrable school walls
where we strained in youth
to create dreams against given odds.
You became Mercury

penning messages to guide us—
weary travellers—
your own path troubled.
No sweet, romantic eulogy can alter
the course taken

as if death were a skin to strip away
and reveal you living.
Soul journeys alone now among elemental forces,
moves to find its way
in the new world of spirits.

ANDREW SALKEY

POEMS

We move now to the Caribbean and to recognizing those continuities of Black literature and culture, continuities between Africa, Black America, and the Caribbean. Andrew Salkey, our next reader, is from Jamaica, the author of several novels, such as A Quality of Violence, Come Home Malcolm Heartland, and a volume of short stories. He's the editor of several important anthologies of African folktales, legends and stories. Andrew Salkey has published volumes of poetry with such striking titles as Hurricane, Earthquake, and many others. He's also the author of several radio plays. He's currently a professor of writing at Hampshire College.

—Ketu Katrak

I SHALL BE READING several poems—four by Caribbean women, two by me, in tribute to James Baldwin. The first poem is by a Jamaican woman called Bridget Jones. "To a Tune by Jimmy Cliff," is the title.

TO A TUNE BY JIMMY CLIFF

So many rivers
When the bamboo sinks
Give me your hand

So many rivers
When the boat is lost
Breathe in the light

So many rivers
When the black rain blows
Shelter me.

The brown water
Returns no dead.

From Cuba, Nancy Morejon.

THE SUPPER

Uncle Juan has come in with his dingy hat
sitting down all full of talk about the blows
his robust body has sustained
blows of the sea and of the heavy sacks
I enter again into the family
saying good afternoon
and fastening on some old household object

I go vaguely looking about the house
picking up the family dog
distracted
searching urgently for my mother's eyes
like the water of every day

Dad comes in later
with his black arms and calloused hands
his sweat-rinsed shirt
that gently threatens to stain my clothes
that's father
bent over
so I could live
and be able to go beyond
where he had been
I stop before the big door
and think
of the war that might break out any minute
but I see only a man who is building
another going by notebook under-arm
and nobody
nobody could resist all this

now we all go tremulous and in good humor
to the table ·
we look at each other later
now we sit in silence
aware that an intrepid star is falling
from the napkins the cups the soup spoons
          from the odor of onions
from the attentive and sad gaze of my mother
who breaks the bread inaugurating night

From Jamaica, Lorna Goodeson with a poem entitled "Keith Jarrett, Rain-maker." And when you hear the phrase "pianoman," please think of "writer-man" in this context, yes? And when you hear "piano," think of "book" or "literature" or "writing."

KEITH JARRETT: RAINMAKER

Pianoman
my roots are african
I dwell in the centre of the sun.
I am used to its warmth
I am used to its heat
I am seared by its vengeance
(it has a vengeful streak)

So my prayers are usually
for rain.
My people are farmers
and artists
and sometimes lines
blur
so a painting becomes a
december of sorrel
a carving heaps like a yam hill
or a song of redemption and wings
like the petals of resurrection
lilies—all these require rain.
So this sunday
when my walk misses
my son's balance on his hips
I'll be alright if you pull down
for me
waterfalls of rain
I never ever thought a piano
could divine
but I'm hearing you this morning
and right on time
it's drizzling now
I'll open the curtains and
watch the lightning conduct
your hands.

And from Trinidad, a poem by Marina Maxwell. It's called "For Denis who was a Drum."

FOR DENIS WHO WAS A DRUM

What can we do
but hold
hope
in this agony,

in this waiting silence,
this tight beginning,
this restructuring
of new pain
for another generation

of birth,
of dying;

what
but love?
And
to love *is* a violence;
love is always a violent understanding.

You heard
the drum,
searching,
inside
your void
and inside
your birthright of terror;

and you named the names
of love, involvement
and commitment
from the chaos.

You shaped love
with both hands,
black and white,
a violent love of understanding.

Yours was an agony
of a torn spirit,
restructuring,
searching,
and always the quick, shy laughter,
the gaiety of being,
the explosion of angered loving.

You chose;
you chose;
you chose
the drum sound:
love is to be a drum,
and love is also a violent dying.

With a mouth,
uncertain
uncertain

in its beginnings,
in its trembling certainty,
a mouth that stamped you, man,
in this three-fingered world;
a mouth that stamped you, black,
in the divisions,
in the shattered concepts
of your accident of birth;
you chose love
and hope
from the gray schizoid murder.

Walk good,
in peace,
in love,
in the drum track of hope.

Beautiful, eh?

The two of my things that I offer—the whole reading is offered as a tribute to Jimmy—but of these two of mine, I did manage to send Jimmy the first one. By the time the second was done, he had died.

JAMES BALDWIN

Thank you for marking the turbulence,
the good fury in the heart of the mountain
that constantly step-shadows weakness
and spikes the spirit to believe
there's a just tomorrow to rely on.

Thank you for narrating the rage
of the people in the ravine
who were pushed down the grieving slide
and whose only continuing loss
is their long credit of patience.

And thank you for signalling the fire
you foresaw when the word
and the iron in it designed so quickly
became skills of furnace response
when the heart of the mountain burst

and the molten truth slashed across America,
as the atavistic cancer burned itself out,
while the new decision sprang loose,
with all the will and all the courage of Cudjoe
and with all the sparkling resolve of revolt.

PRAISE-SONG FOR JAMES BALDWIN

We stare into the near future, like the hurt and
the dying often do, without proclamation.
We see your summons to text and action as a
special healing, a twin annulment of continuing
injury.
When the clarity of self-acknowledgement stretches
its wisdom, a numinous light across a life,
we hear your crisp definitions of your clear candor
catch and hook our scattershot attention,
as if to tell us that your way of gouging reality
is your morning at sea, fresh but edged by salt.

Consider America! In part, yours by right of
seized labour, dispossession, and coffle-old money
you never once had in hand because all that was
bankable was pocketed by allowed thieves.
Again, consider America, where its central dream,
even at night, is as white and out of reach
as sky, and where liberty is on everybody's lips
but equality is seldom ever mentioned,
gospelled only in those voices at the Capitol
gates, led there by the ancestors, time and again!

You always had an accurate, cutting bead on sophis-
try, a straight axe for cant and obfuscation.
Your quick slices across the broad back of *if, but,*
and *perhaps,* all the impossibilities
of stasis that bind us to thraldom, have been the
heralding, swift fires of our time.
Never one for the crusade of emblems and aimless
philosophies, you took to fierce tenderness
like a call to community, wherever it was
threatened by neglect and the emperors of discard.

40

Once you said that miasmal Europe was the spout
that spewed the suffering of modern slavery
in our faces (we make over your words, but not your
intended sense or meaning). Expansion is
as expansion does, and Europe's pillage and suction
have done only Europe good and plenty
and puffed it with surplus, spent on wars,
genocidal compulsion, and on bankrupt morality.
And again you said: so it goes in America, with
its hubris and practised, imperial strut.

We tend to sing our praise-songs only when those we
celebrate have moved well beyond our praise
(and even these words are abjectly late), but
suffice it to say that they are more for us
than we care to know, for those who whistle in
exile, who needle the night into morning,
the ignored at the drag-end of the discouraging
dream, the deprived hurling, their leftover hope
at drift. And that won't do! Better your own
songs than merely our own that ask for closure.

Thank you.

MICHAEL THELWELL

LETTERS FROM DEATH ROW

Our next writer is also from the Caribbean, from Jamaica. Michael Thelwell's most recent book is entitled Duties, Pleasures, and Conflicts: Essays in Struggle, (University of Massachusetts Press, 1987) a collection of essays reviewing and evaluating the civil rights movement over the past twenty-five years. Thelwell's work, his short stories, essays, his novel entitled The Harder They Come, are all a constant reminder to us of the integral connections between culture and politics, between writing and activism. His work with the Student Nonviolent Coordinating Committee (SNCC), in the 1960s, his founding of the Afro-American Studies Department at the University of Massachusetts, and his continuing work against the brutal apartheid regime of South Africa are all part of a life that is dedicated to the cause and the well-being of Black people. Thelwell teaches in the W.E.B. DuBois Department of Afro-American Studies here at the University

—Ketu Katrak

THANK YOU, SISTER. Irie! Give thanks and praises. Jah, Rastafari, dreadful and mighty. I'm going to read in memory of a young man whose life was touched very significantly by most of the writers here, by Chinua, by Jimmy, by Andrew.

In June of '83, I received among my mail a most intriguing letter. It came from Jamaica in a plain envelope, addressed in a hand which I did not recognize. (I'm also reading this because it incorporates many of the themes that James Baldwin represented and many of the issues and the whole question of the presence and meaning of Black people in the world, but in a very particular way). It was addressed in a hand which I did not recognize. It had no return address. Inside was a neatly, elegantly printed letter on ruled notebook paper, but one's eye was immediately caught by the institutional stamp which dominated the top of the page, the purple oval-shaped seal that suggested Victorian bureaucracy. It was from one of the two maximum security prisons in Jamaica, the St. Catherine district prison. It's an ominous towering structure enclosed by high massive stone walls of the kind one associates with medieval fortresses. Built in the 19th century, it is one of the most massive enduring relics left by colonialism in the country. As was to be expected, the letter was a plea for help, but in terms somewhat different than one might have expected.

Rather than summarize, I shall quote the letter, which began with a very polite expression of appreciation of our work in Black Studies and continued, "I am Clinton M.A. Gooden, twenty-three years of age and presently an inmate on death row at the above-mentioned prison. I was innocently convicted for murder after two trials and have lost my appeal to the court all because I am financially incapable of employing a good attorney. But I am still seeking all the help, Mr. Thelwell. I am a past student of Calabar High School and was successful in three subjects at the GCE O-levels; economics, Caribbean history, and religious studies. After leaving school I joined the police force where I spent three years until I was convicted of the murder of another policeman, purely on the basis of circumstantial evidence, which was inconclusive. So, Mr. Thelwell, without help I am a doomed man. My main reason for writing, however, Mr. Thelwell, is to ask your help in the continuation of my studies in history and world affairs. Irrespective of this catastrophic dilemma that surrounds me, I am eager to further my education." [And that's how he came in contact with the Black writers I mentioned. MT] "I would like to keep an open correspondence with you on all aspects of Black history, especially where I'm very backward, on American Black history and Africa itself. Mr. Thelwell, I'm asking you for all the textbooks you can provide to help me. Also, I will help all of us here on death row. On death row, sir, we are being victimized and executed and no chance is given to save the innocent. Capital punishment serves for all those who do not possess capital. Mr. Thelwell, a committee has not made known its report, but every three months men have been hanged. We are suffering and have no-one to help us. Could you, sir, give me and others some educational materials to help us prove to society that we are not recalcitrant slaves and deserve a chance. So, sir, I am trusting that you will respond and generate all the help you can to your unfortunate brothers. I have read that you will be working on a new book about Jamaica's political affairs. I wish you all success. Please give my kind regards to your family and all the lecturers and students at your university. Tell them that all death row inmates would like their help. Yours sincerely, Clinton M.A. Gooden, inmate, Death Row."

It would have been difficult not to have been moved by such a request, or not to be plagued by all the unanswered questions it raised. What was the background of this case? Did it have to do with the political wars that had accompanied the recent election? Books could be sent easily enough, but would the young man still be alive to read them? I knew that the Manley government had suspended executions and set up a commission to study the abolition of the death penalty, but that the new Seaga regime had started to execute some of the backlog of condemned men that had accumulated, as it were, in suspension between life and death. Most troubling of all was how one could respond to the request for books and information without raising unrealistic hopes in the heart of someone who must be clutching at any faint shadow of hope.

In my reply I explained that I had no training in the law and no influence with the authorities there, but that I could and would be willing to supply books and correspond with him on the African and Afro-American situation. I was planning another trip to Jamaica in connection with my work and would try to visit him at that time. In a surprisingly short time, a reply came. He had received the books that I had sent and was already almost finished Chinweizu's *The West and the Rest of Us,* which he said he found instructive, answering a lot of questions for him. It was, he wrote, a great book. He and the other inmates were much taken with the copies of *Drum* magazine, that's a local Black student magazine which I had sent, and again I was impressed with his eagerness to learn and particularly his enthusiasm for information about Black people. As was Andrew Salkey, to whom I showed the letters, who inscribed eight of his own books for inclusion in the next box of books I had selected to take to him. Getting permission to visit the jail was surprisingly easy once I had identified myself as a college professor who was bringing some books on Black history for an inmate. Over the phone the commandant's voice was pleasantly casual: "Well, I suppose that's all right. You can come."

"And will I be able to see him, sir?"

"Yes, that will be possible."

Entering the prison was like stepping back in time. One entered through a small door set in a huge arched iron-ribbed hardwood door set in a huge cut-stone archway that is about 20 feet deep, giving the impression that the entire wall was that thick. The medieval grimness of the entrance evoked descriptions I'd seen of the infamous Elmina Castle in Ghana from which so many of our ancestors had been shipped over to the Americas and slavery. This impression was heightened by a towering, cage-like gate of iron bars enclosing a concrete holding cell from behind which a group of about 30 young Black men stared silently out into the courtyard. The fact that many of them wore only shorts in the afternoon heat only compounded the impression of slavery. Even though I was exactly on time, I was unable to see Gooden. After asking me a few questions, the commandant made a phone call. "A condemned man, Gooden, bring him up." After about fifteen minutes, a longer call, but no Gooden.

"Is there a problem, sir?"

The commandant looked a little embarrassed. The men were complaining. Gooden always called them "the civil servants." The civil servants were complaining. Death row had already been locked down for the day. Getting out one prisoner meant relaxing security for some fifty other condemned men and the warders were unwilling to do that. It was three o'clock in the afternoon. The commandant explained with an embarrassed tone, "Of course, I could order them to bring him, but it would be bad for morale and if anything were to happen . . ." I hastily agreed to come back at a more convenient time. The commandant seemed to appreciate that. He seemed like a very nice man. I left musing on the incident and what it suggested about power, coercion and fear, and the relationship between prisoners and their keepers.

It was three weeks before I was able to get back to the prison, at which time I did see the young man. During the interim, he wrote me three letters which, because I was in Jamaica, I never received until I returned months later to Amherst. Here is one of them: "September 18th. Dear Brother Michael, This is my third letter to you. The previous two I wrote to you to your address at Pelham Road. I am hoping you received them. On a more sour note, I have been informed that you came to visit me, but I cannot see why you were not allowed to see me. I hope you will tell me in your reply. Brother Michael,"—by the way, all these letters are smuggled out—"Brother Michael, my conditions have somewhat deteriorated with the recent upsurge of hangings in Jamaica. One of the men recently hanged was helping himself to my books to study. But I am still alive and continuing to struggle. This magnificent book you have sent me, *From Slavery to Freedom*, is such a remarkable work of Black history in America. It impels me to get to the deepest root of such a study and I am only hoping you will continue to help me. When one reads of Harriet Tubman, that great female fighter against oppression, one cannot just overlook this study. One has to truly go further to find all the facts. Denmark Vesey, Nat Turner, Peter Salem, Frederick Douglass, and all the rest have left a great influence on me. They have taught me the right to struggle, to face oppression, to deploy all the means that are available to me in order to win any successive struggles. I have reached a chapter in *Philanthropy and Self-Help* and I must tell you, Brother, that I am getting my first true study of the famous Booker T. Washington. He is someone who truly fascinates me, truly becoming a Black intellectual. Are there many Black men of this type left? In the era of Reconstruction, the South was really trying to discriminate our race by trying all kinds of stunts in the form of enactments, the Ku Klux Klan and other racist groups. I believe that such conditions have changed. But tell me, Mr. Thelwell, are there still White groups in America that fight racism? And in regard to your home state now, how are conditions? In history, quite a number of activities had taken place there. Are there still relics of slavery in Boston? Brother Michael, in my letter to you last week, I have sent a copy of an article I have sent to *Drum*. I am seeking your comments and hope to contribute more. I will be sending you some songs which have been written by some of us. You can let your students read them if suitable. You are a great friend, my brother, and your book has been widely read by all of us here and we are requesting some of your articles in *Black Scholar* and the rest. I really find great pleasure in corresponding with you and hoping you will be continuing to exchange ideas. Any possible way you can help us is fully accepted, especially if you could send a petition for me to our local privy council asking them to commute my sentence. I am very sorry we did not get to see each other, but hoping you might come to Jamaica again. Give my kind regards to your family and students. And hoping to hear from you soon, your friend, Clinton M. Gooden, inmate, Death Row."

I did not, of course, see this letter until my return to Amherst in December, which explains the look of surprise on Clinton's face as he was marched into the commandant's office a week later without apparently any explanation as to why he was being taken there. There was a new commandant on my second trip. I was careful to get there early in the day and without calling ahead. The new man was even more interesting than the first. When the guards at the gate called, he let me in even though I had no appointment. He was a gaunt, very black man, immaculate in a starched khaki military-style uniform. His bony weathered face, crowned by close-cropped gray hair, gave the appearance of a man who had seen much in a long career spent behind stone walls. I can remember thinking as I looked at the commandant, I wonder what this brother's life has been.

While waiting for Gooden to come I gave him a book, my own, and we chatted about the prison system. The previous decade had seen an unprecedented rise in gun violence in the society. The prisons were full of some 120 men on death row. The prisoners were young, more articulate, and later I learned that there had been a rebellion on death row and Prime Minister Manley had had to interfere. As in all societies, the lowest priority at budget time was the penal system. Then without warning or prompting, the commandant looked intently at me and spoke slowly, choosing his words carefully. "I come from one of the poorest families in Jamaica. I remember what I had to go through, what my family went through. These young boys, they are more educated, more militant. They're not going to accept what I had to accept. And that is why we don't brutalize them." There was a long thoughtful silence and Gooden came. I was very impressed with that statement, quite; I didn't ask for it, I didn't question it, and I felt good about it until some weeks later I met a young man who had just been paroled out of the prison. I described the commandant to him. He said, "Yeah, me know him?", and I told him what he said. "These young men are more militant, they won't take what we had to take, that's why I don't brutalize them."

"Him say that?" He said, "That's the wickedest man God ever make!"

There was a long thoughtful silence, and Gooden came. He came in blinking in the bright sunlight, looking at once apprehensive and hopeful. The warden stopped. The prisoner, a raw-boned athletic-looking youth with wide bony shoulders came to attention and looked at the commandant. "Clinton Gooden, sir," he said, flashing a quick uncomprehending look in my direction. In his first letter he had given his age as twenty-three, but he seemed much younger, no older than sixteen or seventeen. His face was smooth, youthful appearing, unlined and somehow vulnerable. There was no fat on his frame and he seemed physically strong and his eyes were alert, though guarded. His prison-issue white cotton shirt and shorts were crisp and clean. Possibly they had a change before bringing him in. He looked like an eager young freshman, as I profoundly wished he were.

"You have a visitor, Gooden," the commandant said, and the prisoner looked fully at me for the first time, still puzzled.

"You know this man?" the commandant asked.

"No, sir," he said.

I told him my name and he smiled for the first time. They let us talk at a table in the middle of the room. The commandant sat at his desk and did not appear to be listening. The guard stood a few feet away and seemed to be listening very carefully. We sat facing each other across the table, leaning forward so that our faces were only a few inches apart, and spoke quickly in low tones. There was a suppressed liveliness, a quality of energy in him as he quickly told me how he came to be there. He had been posted in a station in the far west of the island. One night, he said, he had returned from an investigation and turned in his gun to the desk officer, gone to the sleeping quarters and gone to bed, only to be wakened by an explosion. He found the desk officer dead. The shot had come from the gun he had just turned in, and even though the entry in the ledger showed that he turned the gun in some half an hour earlier, he was arrested after an investigation. No, he said, there was no history of friction between him and the deceased, nor did the prosecution claim that there was. These facts hardly seemed justification for the bringing of charges, nor could I see how any jury could have convicted a man and seen him sentenced to death on that evidence, and I told him so. Nevertheless, he assured me that that is what happened. In any event, I said, I was not there to retry the case, that was not what my visit meant. I had brought some more books. Was there anything more along those lines that he wished me to do? He told me that some forty to fifty of the condemned men had indicated an interest in the books and wanted a formal course in African and Afro-American history, if I could offer one by correspondence. They were serious and when I said that I was sure I could get my publisher to donate the textbooks, he said that he was sure the inmates could, some of the families had a little money, cover the cost of the books themselves. I agreed that if the permission were granted, myself and members of my department would do it. Once I was back in Amherst, I would start to work on it. He seemed quite pleased and we talked briefly about the books I had with me.

It was with feelings of profound ambivalence that I left the prison. The young man's interest, his excitement about the books and what they had to teach him about his people was palpable and infectious. The interest of the others as he described it was also moving and if the authorities allowed it, the course would, of course, be possible. It was the other expectations that troubled me. The men's sad and rather desperate hope that by demonstrating their receptiveness to education they could favorably impress the authorities and perhaps win some lightening of their sentences, perhaps even save their lives. I thought it unlikely, even in a society whose public rhetoric places such emphasis on the importance of education, that a course in Black history could have that effect on a power structure. But could one expect men, especially young men, in jeopardy of their lives not to clutch at anything even remotely resembling a hope, no matter how ephemeral? I decided that I was a teacher and that if the brothers wanted to study it was my duty to do so, while cautioning them not to invest the undertaking with unrealistic hopes and expectations.

It was December before I was able to get back home and I found a number of letters from the prison awaiting me. Reading them, one could feel, almost visualize, the paradox of the young prisoner's situation. He was reading avidly and intelligently. His imagination flowed. His intellectual horizons and political vision expanded. The books took him into the world and as his mind engaged the present and the past, one could feel in his letters the intellectual excitement that he felt, but his material reality was firmly anchored within the small concrete cell on death row. In November he had come back to Chinweizu's *The West and the Rest of Us*. He wrote, "Brother, my efforts still continue to achieve the ultimate goal of manumitting myself through hard work and study and I am not breaking such a golden opportunity as to study with you. Presently, I'm on the most authentic work of Chinweizu's and it is certainly a true work on the world's problems today. One only has to look at the financial indexes of the industrialized countries and see the downturn that is rapidly taking place." [This was at the end of Mr. Reagan's first term. *M.T.*] "One has to wonder what will become of poor countries in '83. I am not too optimistic about our country's recovery program, because production which stimulates and gives power to development is not here. Our faltering industries are too tied up in North America and these world conditions will only affect the poor of this world. Conditions like these will certainly have an adverse affect on my life. '83 will come with plenty of sorrow, and I'm hoping, Brother Thelwell, that I can survive. Your books have certainly instilled a new dignity, power, and consciousness in my life, and I am glad, Mr. Thelwell. Your visit to me has painted a clear picture for me and I have formed a new zest. With a new year approaching, I hope to work with you more whole-heartedly on any projects you may assign."

In December he wrote about taking his case to the privy council and the possibility of petitioning the government to commute his sentence and about his studies. "My studies are coming along beautiful and I hope you're still bearing my messages about giving me an exam on a syllabus that you will send and then you can grade it to the university level. My life depends on this, Brother. I want to comment today on Africa's military past. I have been studying *The African Genius* by Basil Davidson and it's very interesting, Brother. Let's deal with the Songhai Empire, which started with Sonni. When I read of his military exploits, one is impelled to see that we are men of power and great achievements. Under his military rule, Songhai was prosperous and enjoyed growth in its economy from 1464 to 1492."

Clinton's three letters, almost lost in the accumulated mail of five months, contained the short pieces which appear in an issue of *Drum*. My letter acknowledging his and assuring him that the course would be forthcoming had apparently not reached him by January 17th, when he next wrote. I received that letter in mid-February. It was a good letter, suggesting a quiet determination and mental strength. My heart felt for the young man. He was pursuing whatever channels were open to try to change the situation. "A new year finds me in the same conditions, but I have increased my working effort to liberate myself, Michael. I am working on two fronts: to get the case back in the appellate court, and to ask the governor to commute my sentence. If my forefathers can win freedom from the White slavers, I can also win freedom from my injustice and oppression. Here I also enclose a copy of my article, "Down with Racism in South Africa." I have the pro-foundest revolutionary love for my brothers and sisters there who are struggling to regain their beauty and rights to their homeland. Do you think all of us will unite and love one another as Black to Black? I wrote Mr. Salkey and he wrote back and gave me some of his poems which I find much solace in. He's a good intellectual brother and thanks for mentioning me to him. You are my two great friends. I'm doing a lot of writing, I would like to know if *Drum* will accept some. Do write soon. Love and power, Clinton"

I was happy to write back to tell him that the editors of *Drum* had accepted the articles and that I was in the process of working out the course for him and the brothers. I'm fairly certain he never received that letter because I got one from another prisoner written on March 3rd. It bore no institutional stamp and had been smuggled out. The last paragraph reads, "Charlie Gooden, an ex-cop on death row, asked that I inform you of his predicament. He and a couple of others tried to escape a fortnight ago and the plan blew up. They were caught and beaten with springblades and iron pipes. Gooden is admitted to the public hospital with a broken jaw, a broken spinal cord, a couple of fractured ribs, a broken spleen, and a leg broken in two places being the major injuries. Three of them are admitted to the hospital, Gooden being the worst injured. The warders wanted to kill him, saying he had organized the escape. [Which I can well believe. *M.T.*] I saw them beating him with those iron pipes and springblades from cars."

He subsequently was admitted to the hospital, where he underwent major surgery on four different occasions, acquired himself a girlfriend, wrote me very positive letters. As soon as he was able to walk with the help of crutches and to eat porridge, because his jaw was wired where it was broken, and he never was erect again, he was limp and broken, but they patched him up, at government expense, took six months doing it, and having done that, they hung him.

JOHN EDGAR WIDEMAN

FROM A NOVEL-IN-PROGRESS: "PRESENTS"

Our journey to Africa, to the Caribbean, to Black America now brings us back to the African-American environment and our last writer, one of the most prominent and accomplished of Afro-American writers, John Edgar Wideman. John Wideman is the author of several novels, The Homewood Trilogy, Reuben, Sent For You Yester-day, and the award-winning Brothers and Keepers. He has been described as "the chronicler of Black Pittsburgh." Professor Wideman teaches in the English Department at the University of Massachusetts, and I might add that he is a most welcome addition to our ranks, having seen John's wisdom and his great diplomacy in giving very opportune and useful direction to the English program here at the University. John.

Ketu Katrak

BROTHERS AND SISTERS, it's wonderful to be here this morning. I have enjoyed very much, if enjoy is the right word, I think touched is a better word, the reading of poems and stories by those who preceded me.

I want to share a piece, I think it's going to be part of the novel I'm working on. It's a novel about the fire that occurred in Philadelphia in May of 1985. A bomb was dropped on a rowhouse and eleven people perished, six of them children. I think that's a very crucial event in our history and we can't afford to forget it. And so I'm doing what I think is my bit in trying to keep it alive. One of the characters in the novel is a man who wanders the streets. It's sort of ambiguous where he comes from. He might have been a former college student, he might have simply gone to the university of the streets. He appears in different forms, different versions. One of his names is James Brown, so he may have been a singer at some time, but I'm going to read you a little bit about the origins of this character, one possible origin of this character.

I thought it was also appropriate to read for a few other reasons, well, lots of reasons, but I'll only share a few of them. One is that this is a character who was given a gift, he was given the gift of song. And as I have learned from Chinua Achebe, and from my African ancestors, everything has two sides. A shield, the shield you hold up to defend yourself, even that has a negative side. It can provide a target for your enemy. So all things are good and evil. Good and evil are two sides of the same shield. And so all gifts are also crosses and my character learns that. The segment is called "Presents" and it's about presents that are exchanged. Once in Philadelphia I was listening to the radio and I heard a singer, gospel singer at that time, but he's done popular music as well, named Solomon Burk and he told a story about having received from his grandmother his first instrument, the instrument that started him on his career. And he also said that that same day that she gave him the guitar, she told the story of his life, predicted, told him what was going to happen to him for the rest of his life. And that stuck with me and that's part of this story. "Presents" is also dedicated to Judy, who has given me many presents and whose presence is a gift. And of course we're all standing in the presence, I hope, in some fashion, of James Baldwin. And he would understand this two-sided gift, that his eloquence was not only a source of joy to him.

This is my story. This is my song. Traditional. Hymn. I stood on the bank, oh yes, she said, oh yes, and I did not know what she was yessing any more than I know how her voice, her yes reaches me from wherever she is to wherever I am now, except it's like ships seen from the bank of Jordan in that song, sailing on, sailing on from there to here, quietly as dream, Big Mama, Big Mama, doubling her not because she is not real enough, but because her life takes up so much space. I stare at her, afraid to look away, scared she'll be gone if I do, I'll be gone. Baby, you listen to your Big Mama now, listen 'cause I ain't got nothing but mouth and time, and hardly none that left. He is saucer-eyed, awkward, a big nappy head. She pats each nap and each awakes, a multitude stirring as she passes her old hand once in the air over the crown of his skull. Love Jesus and love yourself and love those who love you, sugar. Those that don't love you don't love theyselves, and shame on 'em. Nobody but Jesus can save their sorry souls. She purses her lips. Her tongue pushes that hard is the world bitter lemon into one cheek. She sucks on it. All the sour of it smears her old lips. She is Big Mama. No bones in her body, even now, even this Christmas so close to death, the bones cannot claim her. Nothing will crack or snap or buckle in her. In her lap he will curl and sleep and always find soft room to snuggle deeper, to fall to sleep. He remembers being big enough to crawl alone under her bed, and little enough—Little sweet doodlebug, you come on over here, give me some sugar—to sit upright and his head just grazes the beehive network of springs, hiding her bed and playing with the dust and light he raises and the tasseled knots of fringed chenille bedspread, high so you had to climb up on her bed. Mind you, don't roll off, boy. He did not think throne, but he knew her bed was raised high to be a special place, to be his Big Mama's bed. So when she kneels beside the bed, he hears the sigh of the room rushing together again over her head, sigh as the fist of her heart, the apron pocket of her chest, empties and fills, the grunt and wheeze of his Big Mama dropping to one knee and lifts the spread and her arm disappears as if she's fishing for him under the bed. Come out, you little doodlebug rascal. I know you hiding in there. Bogeyman get you, you don't come out from under there. Her arm sweeps and he can see her fingers under the edge of the bed inside the cave, though he is outside now and it's like being two places at once, hiding and looking for his own self, watching her old hand, the fingers hooked, beckoning. Come on out, you monkey, you! Sweeping a half-inch off the floor, precisely at the level of the unfailing fringed spread hanging off the side of the bed. What she drags forth this Christmas Eve afternoon, as he watches her kneeling beside the bed, is wrapped in a blanket. Not him this time, but something covered with a sheet and swaddled in a woolly blanket, shape-less. Then Big Mama digs into folds and flaps, uncovers woman curves, the taut shaft. There are long strings and a hole in the center. Gently as she goes, she cannot help accidents that trick stirrings from the instrument, a bowl of jelly quivering. Perhaps all it needs is the play of her breath as she bends over it, serious and quiet as a child undressing a doll, or the air all by its own self is enough to agitate the strings when Big Mama finally has it laid bare across the bed. The story, as he's preached it so many times since, is simple. A seven-year-old boy makes his grandmother a song. He intends to sing it for her Christmas Day, but Christmas Eve afternoon she calls him into her bedroom and kneels and pulls a guitar wrapped in rags and blankets from under her bed. He is mesmerized and happy. He hugs his Big Mama and can't help telling her about the love song he's made up for her Christmas present. She says, "You better sing it for me now, baby." And he does, and she smiles the whole time he sings. Then she lays out the sad tale of his life as a man. He'll rise in the world, sing for kings and queens, but his gift for music will also drag him down to the depths of hell. She tells it gently, he is only a boy, with her eyes fixed on the ceiling and they fill up with tears. Oh yes, oh yes, yes, yes, Jesus. The life he must lead a secret pouring out of her, emptying her. Already she is paying for the good and evil in him. Yes, yes. She is quiet then, still. They sit together on the side of her high bed till it's dark outside the window. He can't see snow but smells it, hears how silently it falls. She asks him, "Sing my song one more time," his little Christmas gift song because he loves to sing and make rhymes and loves his Big Mama, and the grace of sweet Jesus is heavy in this season of his birth. By the next morning, his Big Mama is dead. The others come for Christmas Day and discover her. He's been awake since dawn, learning to pick out her song quietly on his new guitar. His mother and the rest of them bust in, stomp their snowy shoes in the hallway, and Merry Christmas! and Where's Big Mama? They find her dead in bed and he's been playing ever since. Everything she prophesied right on the money, honey, to this very day. He's been up and he's been down and that's the way she told him it would be all the days of his life, amen. Each time, in the middle of the story, he thinks he won't ever need to tell it again. Scoot it up under the skirt of Big Mama's bed. His mother comes over to visit and she fusses at him. "You're too big a boy to be hiding-go-seek under Mama's bed. Don't let him play under there, Mama. Don't baby him. Time he start growing up." His mother visits and takes a bath in Big Mama's iron tub. He sees her bare feet and bare ankles, her bare butt as he holds his breath and quiet as a spider slides to the edge and peeks up through the fringy spread. He lifts the covering to see better, inch by inch, quiet as snow. She has a big round behind with hairs at the bottom. He thinks of watermelons and can't eat that fruit without guilt ever after. He watches her as she stands in front of the mirror of his grandmother's chiffoniere. His heart beats fast as it can. He's afraid she'll hear it, afraid she'll turn quickly and find his eye peeking up from under the covers at her. But when she does turn, it's slowly, slowly, so he hears the rub of her bare heel on the linoleum where the rug doesn't stretch to where she's standing. He drops the window of his hiding place, he's spared a vision of the front of her, titties, pussycat between her legs, just ankles and bare feet until she's finished and wrapped in one Big Mama's housecoats and asking for him in the other room. "You been in here all this time? You been hiding under there while I was dressing? Why don't you say something, boy?" The story has more skins than an onion, and like an onion it can cause a grown man to cry when he starts to peeling it. Or else it can go quick. Big Mama said, "That's the most beautiful song in the world. Thank you, precious. Thank you and thank Jesus for bringing such a sweet boy to this old woman."

"Will you teach me how to play?"

"Your old grandmama don't know nothing 'bout such things. She's tired, besides. You learn your own self. Just beat on it like a drum till something come out sound good to you. The music's in the box, like the sword in the stone. Beat it, pound it, chisel it, then one day gon' sound good. Gon' slide loose easy as it slided in. Then it's smooth as butter. Then it sings God's praise, oh yes, oh yes. She gave him the guitar in Jesus' name, amened it, prayed over it with him that Christmas Eve afternoon how many years ago. Well, let's see. I was seven then, and I'm an old man now, so that's, that's how long it's been. That's how many times I've preached the story. My grandmother believed in raising a joyful noise unto the Lord, tambourines and foot-stomping and gut-bucket piano rolls and drums and shouts and yes, if you could find one, a mean guitar, rocking like the ark in heavy seas till it gets good to everybody, past the point of foot patting and finger popping in your chair, past that till the whole congregation out they seats, dancing in the air. Something born that day, and something died. His fate cooked up for him like a mess of black-eyed peas and ham hocks and he's been eating at the table of it ever since. Lean days and fat days. Where did she find a guitar? Who'd played the instrument before it was his? Could it ever be his if other fingers had plucked its strings, run up and down the long neck, grease and sweat ground into its wood, its metal strings. When he was at last alone with the gift she'd given him and told him not to play till Christmas, he peered into the

hole in its belly, held it by its fat hips and shook it to hear if anybody'd
left money in there. If the right sound won't come out plucking it, there
was always the meaty palm of his hand to knock sense into it. How
long did he hide in the church before he carried his box out on the
street corner? How long for the Lord, how many licks for the Devil?
How long before you couldn't tell one from the other? Him the last to
know, always. A boy wonder, an evil hot-blood Buddy Bolton Willie
the Lion Robert Johnson wildman boy playing the fool and playing the
cowboy fool shit out that thing, man. Yes, oh yes. And one day, praise
God, I said, "Huh-uh. No more. Thank you, Jesus. And broke it over my
knee and cried because I'd lost my Big Mama."

Atlantic City. Niggers pulling rickshaws up and down the boardwalk. No, if I'm lying I'm flying.

They did, boy?

Yes, yes, they did. Dragging White folks around behind 'em in these
big carts, like in China, man, or wherever they keep them things. Saw
that shit on the boardwalk in Atlantic City in the U.S. of A. Yeah. And
niggers happy to be doing it, collecting fabulous tips, they said. Haul-
ing peckerwoods around. Not me, see, I knew better. I'd seen the
world, had me a gig in one of them little spliff clubs on Arctic Avenue,
enough to keep me in whiskey. Didn't need a pad, it was summer.
Sleep on the beach or sleep with one of the ladies dig my plan, a real
bed, a shower every few days to scald the sand out my asshole. Living
the life, partner, till I woke up one morning in the gutter. Stone gutter,
man, like a dead rat. Head busted, vomit all over my clothes. In broad
daylight I'm lolling in the gutter, man. Said, huh-uh. No indeed. These
the bonds of Hell. Done fell clean off the ladder and I'm down in the pit.
The goddamn gutter floor of the pit's bottom. I'm lost. Don't a living
soul give one dying fuck about me and I don't neither. That's when I
hollered, Get me up from here, Big Mama. You said I'd rise, and I did.
You prophesied I'd fall and here I am. Now reach down and help me
up. Give me your soft silk purse old woman's hand and lift this crusty
burden off the street. Take me back to your bosom. Rise and fall, you
said. Well, I can't fall no further, so carry me on up again. Please, please
Big Mama, reach down off that high side of your bed and bring me
back. Her fingers hooked like an eagle's beak, holding a cloak of
feathers fashioned from wings of falling angels. Where you find this,
Big Mama? How'm I supposed to play this thing? Beat it, you say?
Pound it like a drum? Just step out in the air with it round your
shoulders, let the air take you and fly you on home. Squeeze it till it
sounds like you need it to sound. Good. Giant steps ain't nothing if
they ain't falling up and falling down and carrying you far from this

place to another. Sailing. To meet me in the morning on Jordan one day, singing. Yes, oh yes. I stood on the bank and my neck ached like I'd been lynched. Like I'd been laid out for dead and hard rock was my pillow and cold ground my bed. Hard rock my pillow and help me today, help me tell it. I scrambled to my feet and shook the sooty graveclothes and sand and scales and dust and feathers and morning blood off my shoulders, skinny as a scarecrow, funky as toejam, my mouth dry and my eyes scored by rusty razors, my tongue like a turtle forgot how to poke his head out his shell. Scrambled to my aching feet and there it was, spread out over me, the city of my dreams, Philadelphia, all misbegotten and burnt crisp and sour, sour at the roots as all my bad teeths. Play it, son. Buck a doo. Buck a little dee. Black is sugar burnt to the bottom of a pan and Big Mama told me, she said, squeeze it to the last drop. A simple story, easy to tell to a stranger at the bar who will buy you a drink. Young boy and old woman, Christmas time, reading each other's minds, exchanging gifts of song, his fortune told, the brief bright time of his music, how far it took him, how quickly gone, the candle flaring up, guttering, gone. He told it many times, risen, fallen, up, down, rubs his crusty eyes and peers into a honey-colored room with no walls. Feet scurry past his head, busy going every which way. Sandals and brogans and sneakers and Stacy Adams and the pitter-pat of high-stepper high heels on the pavement as he lifts his head and goes over the whole business again, trying to settle once and for all who he must be and why it always ends this way, his head on the hard rock of curbstone, the ships sailing on, sailing on. The Schulkill River is brass or blood or mud, depending on the day, the season, the hour. Big Mama is where she is, he is here, her voice plain as day in his ear. He wishes someone would pat him on his head and say, everything's gonna be alright.

PANEL
DISCUSSION

GOOD AFTERNOON and welcome again to this, the final session of a conference that was conceived twice. First, to be a celebration of the presence of James Baldwin and Chinua Achebe in our midst, and secondly, when it was not possible, because James Baldwin was no longer with us, a reconception that's cast itself in the form of a tribute to James Baldwin.

The conference was started last night with a speech by Chinua Achebe which he called "Spelling our Proper Name." He said of Jimmy Baldwin, "Baldwin wants to lift from the backs of Black people the burden of their race" and that he "wrestled to unmask the face of his oppressor, to see his face and to call him by name." James Baldwin said to us, "Go back to where you started or as far back as you can. Examine all of it. Travel your road again and tell the truth about it. Sing or shout or testify or keep it to yourself, but know whence you came." This morning we heard Black writers tell us through their works whence they came. This afternoon we make a tribute to James Baldwin, each in his own way, as to how James Baldwin's work, how James Baldwin's presence, how James Baldwin the writer affected their lives. At lunch today, John Wideman said he was reminded by this morning's session of a song that we used to sing called "I'll Be Somewhere Listening." We hope—we know—that Jimmy is somewhere listening. It's my great pleasure to introduce Black writers who perhaps have travelled their roads again, but certainly by this morning's performance convinced us that they know whence they came. We have no particular order except this—I am commanded that we begin with John Wideman and that we end with Chinua Achebe, and whatever happens between that is up for grabs between Mike Thelwell and Irma McClaurin-Allen . . . John.

—Esther Terry

WIDEMAN: There'll be lots to grab, don't worry, don't worry, not to worry. I just want to signify a little bit. This is not a critical paper, this is a practice that comes from the folk and comes from the tradition and it's called signifying. And it's a kind of riffing and improvisational talk that has a logic, and if it's done well it has six or seven levels of logic and double meaning and inference and it's also a way of talking about somebody like a dog. And so—and like a monkey—or you're the monkey if you're doing the signifying and you make a monkey out of someone else. But I just want to throw out a couple words and a couple of concepts and I'm sure they'll be taken up with force and eloquence by brothers and sisters. And I hope for you also, because at some point we can make this a discussion I'm sure that includes more than simply the voices here.

So signifying. Think about the word "letters." That's the text. Letters. How will letters impact upon Afro-American tradition? Well, in many ways, for instance, a watermelon is a letter from home. A watermelon is a letter from home. And that takes me back to growing up in Pittsburgh. When I grew up in Pittsburgh, I didn't know anything about literature. I didn't know anything, at least I didn't think I knew anything, about the possibility of earning a livelihood or earning respect through an academic enterprise or through writing books. Those things were not part of my life. People around me read, but those books seemed to come from somewhere else. They weren't produced in my neighborhod. There weren't writers on the street. I'd never met a writer. I knew I loved language, people around me told wonderful stories, so I had a feel for the language and an interest in it, but no way to focus it in terms of a literate tradition, letters, which is another meaning, of course, of letters. Literacy, the ability to read.

So into that world came the figure of James Baldwin and that was so important for me because what that signified, what that meant was that a Black person could be a writer. After that, it doesn't take a rocket scientist to make the connection. If he or she can do it, and they're the way I am, they're like I am, well, then maybe I can do it, too. And so the importance of that inspiration is basic, is fundamental. Now I was very lucky because growing up as a kid I had the figure of Baldwin to relate to, just to open up the door. And then here, forty odd years later, I met the man and had a chance to be in his presence, and so I owe a tremendous debt to the example of his work implicitly and explicitly. What he says in his work about the craft of writing, I learned from. The quality of the writing, I learned from. His ability to take those oral traditions and that folk wisdom that was part of my life in Pittsburgh and make that into serious literature, that all was important.

But I want to signify a little more on letters and literacy. Of course, literacy and letters were our, Black people's, way into the European mind as real people. That was a door we had to come through. We had to prove we could write and that meant we were human beings. Now that was a real stupid game, but we played it, and we did it, so letters go back to that. Letters in another sense became crucial in the actual exploration and the production of Afro-American writing. Letters, of course we had to put our words, our oral literature, into letters as well as become literate. But then letters, those pieces of communication, one person to another, things that are written with postscripts and prescripts and all that, those are letters also, aren't they? And the earliest Black writing was surrounded by letters from Massa So-and-so and Mister So-and-so, who said this slave is okay. This slave in fact was born in Alabama and so his story is true. And these letters of attestation were our entitles. Of course entitles are another kind of letter. Alphabet. Initials. Letters. My grandfather always called me John Edgar. Why? Because those were my actual names and I was entitled to those names and he knew that there was some kind of authority, some kind of power. Because people didn't call him by his name. They called him whatever they wanted to call him. So he wanted to make sure that two generations later, his grandson had as many names as I was entitled to. And after the period of slavery, people took on lots of names. George Washington Carver Madison Jones. Why? Because they were entitled to names and they wanted those names. Letters. Names.

And in the production of literature, we use the epistolary form, in many of our important works. Think of Jimmy Baldwin's letter in *Fire Next Time* to his nephew. Think of Alice Walker using the epistolary form in *The Color Purple*. Think of the letters back and forth from Black people in exile who are trying to stay in touch, trying to move. Think of the famous letters from the early abolitionist writers. So the letter form itself is something that is germane to the tradition. Now think of what a letter is. What a letter is. It's an attempt by one person to communicate a message to another. The form has certain qualities in it that begin to have a logic of their own, just the form itself. Because think of what happens when you write a letter. When you write a letter, you not only perform an act of self-revelation, but you are simultaneously making somebody else, you're making your correspondent by what you choose to say and how you say it—your form of address—you're really creating the person on the other end also. And that's what's so beautiful about James Baldwin's letter in *Fire Next Time*, because he's telling who he is through these words, through these letters, in this letter. But he's also making that nephew into a special kind of person. So we see the power of letters in that sense. The power of written communication, the intensity.

And we think about this a little more. Isn't that the form of literary criticism? Isn't literary criticism in a funny way a kind of open letter to an author? It's addressed to his book or her book, something they have done, and it's a discourse, a dialogue between the critic and the writer. And the same thing obtains there that obtains in personal communication, because the critic is making the book by the form of the letter and what he or she chooses to say.

And now I draw back, now I draw back, because there is a form of letter that seems to be appearing like letters appear in some of Garcia-Marquez' wonderful stories, just overnight. One appears and then it's like a whole snowfall, these letters and posters are all over the place. Here we're getting a species of letter which endangers my relationship to James Baldwin and James Baldwin's relationship to the tradition and to you and to your children, etc. And this kind of letter—two quick examples. There was a letter published in *Esquire* magazine from Peter Hamill to a Black friend. Now with friends like that, who needs enemies, because if you read that letter, you can see the kind of person that Hamill created through his letter, what he communicated about the recipient of this letter. And also it's more about himself. And then I have in front of me a letter addressed to Julius Lester. This appeared in a newspaper in Boston, a letter to Julius Lester from a friend whose name is Marty Goldman. And I put these two letters together, they just happen to be the ones that come to mind. There are lots of other examples, but it's the kind of letter that's important, because it's a poison pen letter. It's a critique, it's a review, it's a way of creating a personality and a person which we have no authority for except the letter writer's version encapsulated in that form of letter. And it has certain qualities which I want you to be aware of so when you see another one of these letters you'll know what to do with it.

There's a myth being promulgated in these kinds of letters. It's a myth about some glorious time in the 60s when Blacks and Whites got along very well and don't you remember, my friend, how wonderful things were then, is one part of the address. Another part of it is, you know, things are a lot better than they were in slavery days, and you know, some of your brothers and sisters don't even appreciate that, and of course we do. That's another part of the letter. Then there's another part that's something like this: We are the elect and the elite because we do recognize this former period of brotherhood and how things are getting better all the time. Now this letter can be addressed to a Black friend, but a picture is being formed of that correspondent, and inside the letter there are characters. And I think, unfortunately, James Baldwin will become, and has already become in the two letters I'm talking about, a kind of villain. Because he embodies all those, to the writer, those negative qualities. He does not appreciate progress. He is enraged and bitter. He lost his footing as an artist and simply became a propagandist. And that version of Baldwin's career is very dangerously being promulgated and it's being pushed in a kind of surreptitious way by these letters.

All I want to say is that, in sort of conclusion and passing it on, I really don't have a conclusion. I really simply wanted to bring certain things to your attention and remind myself, remind you that we have a responsibility. That Baldwin's writing, in a sense anybody's writing, is never, it never creates closure. It's active, it's alive. And we have to take the responsibility, bear the responsibility of repeating those words in a way that makes sense, in a way that makes sense to the heart and to the mind. Keeping them alive and passing them on as teachers, as letter writers, as literate people, as writers ourselves.

McCLAURIN-ALLEN: In some ways we have here a tapestry, part of which you heard today, sort of coming from all aspects of the diaspora. I'd like to think in terms of a tapestry, and Wideman has just sort of thrown out one strand and I'd like to sort of throw out another. It seems to me that in some ways a tapestry might be an apropos symbol of James Baldwin's life. I remember seeing lots of people around here, lots of different people, all with different ideas, different agendas, and somehow he managed to bring all of those people together; or one can think in terms of texts and subtexts, you know, as part of a kind of dominant discourse, that discourse being James Baldwin's life, and that each of us speak to that. And what I'd like to do is sort of address, maybe not directly, but in some ways tangentially, some of the issues that Wideman has talked about and talk about the impact of James Baldwin on my writing.

In 1971, I was 10,000 miles away from home in the former British colonial army town of Kuna, India, when I first became acquainted with James Baldwin. Not in the flesh, of course, that privilege was not to be mine for another thirteen years, but through his writings, through that which was both his sword and his shield. Language. To a young Black girl of nineteen years old, disenchanted with her country and unsure of her place in the unfolding drama of Black liberation, Baldwin's words were a map. They spoke direction, guidance. For a struggling Black writer who had escaped to India because the landscape of middle America liberal White midwestern Iowa college town was too foreign and too alien, Baldwin's words were solace. Validation that I did not need to become a shadow tap-dancing in cornfields in order to write. The source of my writing was not Iowa, but Chicago. The west side of Chicago, full of housing projects, dark alleys, pee-stained stairways, pregnant young girls, leering old winos, angry mothers, prying social workers, friendly junkies, and brooding police. Those were the images of my poetry, poems which did not fit into the prescribed boundaries laid out for me in L-I-T-E-R-A-T-U-R-E, literature at Grinnell College. In Baldwin I found a place to be and he spoke to me.

"One writes out of one thing only, one's own experience. Everything depends on how relentlessly one forces from this experience the last drop, sweet or bitter, it can possibly give. This is the only real concern of the artist, to recreate out of the disorder of life that order which is art." My time spent in India was most difficult. I, too, was "a stranger in the village," unaccustomed to the overt hostility and painful curiosity that accompanied my presence. Yes, I had been born and reared in the United States, and yes, I had heard of racism, but no-one had ever been so hostilely curious about me before. The enfolding despair at being seen as not human, but rather "a living wonder," as Baldwin talks about, came not only from how my hair was seen as novelty, as Baldwin notes in his essay, "Stranger In the Village," in which he says, "Some thought my hair was the color of tar, that it had the texture of wire, or the texture of cotton." It emerged from the refusal of many to recognize my humanity. Only when I spoke and was marked as an American did I have any identity at all. Then I gained immediately entry to places where my African brothers and sisters could not go. All of this, in addition to the rock-throwing, provoked a tremendous rage. And, as Baldwin wrote, "the rage of the disesteemed is personally fruitless, but it is also absolutely inevitable." My sense of indignation was even greater because my affronters were brown and black, like me. I painfully and personally witnessed the tragedy of colonialism. My single refuge from the dissonance of attitudes shaped by a history of British colonialism in India lay in Baldwin's presagement in the last line of "Stranger In the Village": "This world is white no longer, and it will never be white again."

The discovery of this small book, *Notes of a Native Son,* spoke so essentially to my sense of discourse, it enabled me to survive the Bangledesh war in India, and inevitable rites of passage of an Afro-American coming of age. Baldwin gave me sanctuary. Upon return to the United States, I immersed myself in the study of Black literature, which heretofore had remained unrevealed. I was convinced that I could follow the prescription implicit in Baldwin's life and his writing: "It is the part of the business of the writer to examine attitudes, to go beneath the surface, to tap the source." Today, as a Black female writer, I sense Baldwin's presence, indelible, upon the conscience of White America and the souls of Black folk. He was not only, he was not the only writer of significance for those of us born during the civil rights era and weaned on the struggle for liberation that exploded in the 1960s, but without a doubt his courage to be "a public witness" helped forge the space and clarify the context in which we now live and create our art. He spent his life contesting the boundaries of racism and defining what it meant to be human. It is a prodigious legacy. The battle to be "honest and a good writer," as James Baldwin defined both, still rages. I am forever endebted.

One of the things that struck me as we were talking over lunch and listening to Wideman not talk formally about Baldwin, but sort of raise a lot of different issues, I was thinking about how to respond, how to sort of pick up on that and all I can do is, in a sense, go to the source and what I'd like to do is sort of take up on the idea that he'll be somewhere listening. That somewhere Baldwin is listening, and this is for Jimmy, from the source. (Singing]—*One of these mornings, and it won't be very long, you gonna look for me and I'll be gone home, 'cause I'm going to a place where there's nothing, nothing to do, and I'm gonna walk around Heaven all day.* So wherever Baldwin is listening, peace be still.

THELWELL: I once had a very good student who was White who was headed towards graduate school to pursue a Ph.D. in literature and I got a letter from her which was a kind of unsettling letter, if you made your living from the pursuit of literature, which said, I'm going to work for AT&T. I think graduate school can wait because I have concluded, she wrote, that literature is not a suitable occupation for a grown person. And knowing what goes on in those graduate schools of literature, I had to agree with her. And what Jimmy Baldwin did and what Chinua Achebe did for my generation was to restore some of the luster to the occupation, to restore some of the seriousness, to restore some of the high purpose. Because literature, as practiced in circles of White folk in this country and in Europe, and the practice of literary criticism even worse has been so debased, has been so cheapened, that it has been reduced to irrelevance. And if there's anybody in this room who don't believe me, correct me. Point out to me a writer out of White culture who has affected anything in our time, or a novel.

But literature cannot be divorced from morality. It cannot be divorced from struggle, it cannot be divorced from history. There's a curious way in which history throws up the figures, gives birth to the creatures that will in turn define history. My generation, our generation, was a most momentous and consequential one in the history of Black people. When I was a young man, Africa became independent, threw off nearly a hundred years of alien imposition, colonial rule, and the ravaging and disparaging of its cultures. In my generation, I will always be gratified and grateful that I was given the historical opportunity to play a small role in that. Black people in this country rose up and threw off a hundred years from the end of Reconstruction of racist subjugation and the disparagement of their culture, their identity, the reduction of their presence and the elimination of their future and their aspirations. Now you don't have two such movements, and they fed each other, they weren't independent of each other, it was part of the same struggle, you don't have two such movements taking place without extraordinary and profound consequences. But you also don't have such a movement taking place on a political front unless there are intellectual warriors helping to define and crystallize the consciousness. Because what we're talking about is uncertainty, what we're talking about is change. We're talking about events, the consequences of which are not known. We're talking about events which even as you live them you don't fully understand. And it is because history has really deprived White people in the West, maybe White people in Russia and White people in South Africa have similar challenges, but deprived them of that opportunity, that their literature is so bankrupt.

Well, this opportunity and this challenge was given to the Black world and it certainly is true that in the movement, as we tried to engage the complex and dangerous issues of social change, it was that luminous and vibrant voice of James Baldwin, that extraordinary intelligence, who, coming out of the depths of Black culture and experience in this country, whose prose voice in its lambency was a distillation of the very best of Black culture expression, the blues, the spirituals, the Bible, the gospel, the song sermon, the grim and bitter experience of Africans in this country. And the knowledge and wisdom gained therefrom. And he could, in his genius, or, as my brother, my elder and senior and respected brother Chinua said, the prodigality of his talent, refine three hundred years of Black experience, wisdom, learning lessons, and suffering into an instrument of struggle. So that for the first time in any real way in the history of this country, in the history of this sorry republic, the voice and weight and momentum of the Black experience addressed this nation directly and it flayed and it lacerated and it inspired and it challenged. And, as Esther said at another occasion, that was the inspiration, that was the shield and the armor that we took with us into struggle. But you can't talk about where Black people are in this country, my brother, without talking at least as much again as to where White people was. And Jimmy Baldwin single-handedly did it, by the fearlessness of the way he engaged, and his anchorage in, truth, Jimmy spoke the truth. He once said at Howard University, we must speak the truth till we can no longer bear it, and that's what he did. Between his intelligence and his honesty and his commitment to truth and struggle, and the extraordinary scintillating brilliance of his prose, Jimmy bestrode the literary world in this country and restored a measure of relevance, of dignity, of power to the literary profession, which had become trivialized.

And helped us liberate ourselves. And he didn't talk only about race. He talked about sex. Sex and race, the two taboos of this puritanical culture. And he talked about them openly and honestly and he cleared the way. He cleared the way and he elevated our consciousnesses. It was an unusual disposition of genius, of talent, of character, of courage combined in the small frame and the luminous eyes and extraordinary visage of James Arthur Baldwin. It was a gift. It was also a burden because unlike any number of writers I could mention who are confused about their responsibility, James Baldwin always knew, always knew that that extraordinary and prodigious gift given him by the ancestors and by history, and that opportunity, carried a burden and responsibility that he was not about to give up. And it was very instructive to me as a young man to watch that process, starting out by simply being mesmerized by his brilliance and his clarity and his fearlessness and his courage. Taking him in a certain way into oneself. And you knew, as the Igbo ancestors say, that as a man dances, so the drums are beaten for him. And Jimmy was leading these crackers a furious dance. He was going to the very heart of the cultural assumptions of supremacy and racism in the country and he went there fearlessly so that American culture had to cope with him in one way or another.

First they tried praise and bribery and took him into the circle of their prominent intellectuals and writers. And one could as a young man in the dormitories at Howard University, see him on these television talk shows, with all these "intellectuals" as they tried to resolve him into their circle. What are you angry about, Jimmy? You made it, you're big time now. Jimmy, you're a celebrity. Jimmy, you're a searing genius. And they thought that in Jimmy's hands the literary undertaking was, in the words of one of them, making it, to project oneself forward. But Jimmy understood that writing was better than that, more than that, that in point of fact what he represented with the prodigality of his gifts and his abilities was nothing less than the distilled essence of Black experience and the unfinished struggle. So he could never become a part of them. And it was precisely in one of the most brilliant documents of American theater, which addresses among other things not just racism, but the limitations of liberalism, *Blues for Mr. Charlie,* that they turned on him with a venom and have attempted ever since to dismiss his work. They said he had dissipated his talents in rage and bitterness. What Jimmy taught me and every Black writer is this: you cannot address your work to that culture or to those people. It has to come out of the Black experience and be addressed to them. Who wants to participate, fine. But the moment it became clear that Jimmy could not become their court jester, that Jimmy could not become their apparatchik, that Jimmy would not dance to any tune that played in search of praise and preferment, they turned against him.

And that story is instructive. I mean the details of it I'm putting together now, of how the literary establishment turned against and tried to destroy the accomplishment, the extraordinary heritage that James Baldwin left to us, because what he did in forty-five years of writing, what he did was to change forever in this country the inflated, self-serving, complacent and racist terms of discussing the racial realities and histories of this country. He deprived this culture of the kind of smug complacent assumptions based on the innate superiority of White genes, culture, and history, and said huh-uh, there is another voice here. There is another reality, you're going to have to face that. Richard Wright said that literature is really a struggle over the definition of reality and after James Baldwin's contributions, the nature of American reality, the nature of the perception, the terms of that perception have changed forever. And he has left us therefore a basis to advance the struggle, to continue the discourse.

I could stop there, but I'm not going to. You'll have to bear with me for a minute. Because interestingly enough, in a quite different historical context, but with many of the cultural dynamics being very similar, another voice, a 26-year-old Igbo man, raised up a song and a chant when the British instrutor said, well, if you don't like this African character, create your own. I don't know if that instructor is around or he knew what he created, but when he threw out that challenge, *Things Fall Apart* was the consequence. And since, you know, I'd been around Baldwin so long, been exposed to him so long, been influenced by him so long, and really patterned, really patterned my career, and by that I don't mean career, I mean what it means to be a writer on those few occasions when I do write, on his splendid example, it wasn't so dramatic to me. But as a young Black man seriously, so I thought, involved in struggle and knowing that my antecedents were African and liking literature, I tried to read all the African literature I could get. And stopped, because what was being called African literature was not. It was colonial literature. It was literature set in Africa, written by White tourists. And the African presence and reality was always peripheral, always distorted, picturesque, strange and exotic. And I hadn't understood that as clearly as I just said it, but I do know that I had a profound dissatisfaction with everything I could get my hands on to read about Africa. Till one sunny afternoon I picked up a little volume called *Things Fall Apart* and two pages into the book, I was whooping and hollering. The other person in the house was Stokely Carmichael. He goes, "Nigger, has you gone crazy?" I said, no, I ain't gone crazy, brother, but I want you to see this, because all of a sudden I begin to understand everything I'd been looking for. I begin to hear the voice and the timbre and the tones and the density and the reality and the values of Black people's experience in history. I have suddenly encountered for the first time in my life a Black novel.

Now that was very dramatic, an African novel. Now that was very dramatic because of the historical context. It also affected my life in ways I can't demonstrate, because I have since that time devoted the next twenty-five years to the study, in a desultory kind of way, but it's been continuous, of traditional African cultures. And I have a much better sense of the forces and the constructs and the values which produced my ancestors and therefore me. And that lifelong interest and study was generated by reading that one book. It's not so sharp and clear in Jimmy Baldwin's case, but it is equally definitive. If you look at how we write today, if you look at how we understand ourselves today, I can't point exactly to *The Fire Next Time*, or *Notes of a Native Son*, or *Nobody Knows My Name*, maybe, but somewhere in there, that body of work of Jimmy's was just as effective, just as changing, just as fundamental, and therefore just as revolutionary as Chinua's example. And to have had the benefaction of being able to be associated with those two men, who have changed the intellectual tides of the century. That's what they have done.

Changed the way Black people understand themselves and how they engage the problems that they will have to continue to engage. Epochs of profound historical change and conflict create figures of that kind. We are all of us not only the beneficiaries, the beneficiaries of not only the historical and political struggle, we are the beneficiaries of the literary legacy and example of these two giants. Thank you.

ACHEBE: Thank you, Michael. Thank you, John, thank you, Irma. This is the third time in twenty-four hours that I am making a public statement on Baldwin. And the fourth time since he died. That's a lot of times. And so, if I repeat myself, I hope you don't mind.

In 1983, in Gainesville, Florida, I met Baldwin for the first time in person. That meeting was very dramatic. I had known of him and read him and admired him for at least twenty years before then. In fact, when I read *Go Tell It on the Mountain* in Nigeria, in the 60s, I went on to the American Information Service Library, whatever it was called, to see if there were other books by him or by people like him. And they didn't have any books by him or anybody like him. They had no Richard Wright, they had nothing at all in that line. And so I made a suggestion that they should consider bringing in such books, and they did. I was so moved by *Go Tell It on the Mountain* and as it happened, after that I read Joyce Cary's last novel. (Joyce Cary was, perhaps, was certainly one of the great, one of the leading English novelists of this century, who had written some really great books, including *The Horse's Mouth, Herself Surprised,* and so on, but he began with a very bad book, which was set in Nigeria, it was called *Mr. Johnson.*) This book set in Nigeria was the beginning of my interest in Joyce Cary. So I read everything else he wrote. Now his last book—I think it was called *Not Honor More*, which he didn't really quite finish, I think it was sort of in the last stages before he died—when I read this book, it was so like *Go Tell It on the Mountain*, the inspiration seemed to me to be the same and I was alarmed, I was concerned. And I said I hope Baldwin had not read this book. And so I rushed, this was the level of my concern, I rushed to the library to check the dates. And I was, you can't imagine the relief I felt when I saw that Baldwin had published years before Joyce Cary. And I'm convinced, I'm not a scholar in this kind of way, but I'm convinced that Joyce Cary had read *Go Tell It on the Mountain*. But that was the level of my identification with this man I'd never met.

And so when I met him in Gainesville, Florida, in 1983, I said, "Mr. Baldwin, I presume." And he was absolutely delighted with that. That occasion was also memorable in another sense. We had both been invited by the African Literature Association Conference to open their annual conference that year with a conversation. This conversation was marred, was destroyed, by somebody, some unknown voice from somewhere in Gainesville, Florida, getting into the circuit of the public address system and while Baldwin was talking on the platform, this voice began to pour in racist abuse. And it was a most terrifying experience. This huge hall, absolutely packed full, this thing happening, and I saw tough Black people in the audience rush out to the doors to take possession of this room. It was like an invasion. And Baldwin took this in his stride. He waited for a moment, then he began to talk to this voice.

That was my first meeting with him and I was hoping this year that we were going to meet again, this was one of the reasons I came here, this was the arrangement. Now I have read some commentaries by people who don't seem to understand the meaning of Baldwin and there is this suggestion that perhaps the whole Baldwin phenomenon is some kind of trick. Somebody's playing a trick somewhere, there's, you know, why is this, why is everybody talking about him? What's there? What's this? And there's no trick. The difference, I think Mike has mentioned, brought this out very clearly, the difference between what Baldwin stood for and what so many other people stand for is a difference in seriousness. Baldwin was able to combine three elements: talent, passion, and morality. I don't mean Sunday School morality, that's not what I'm talking about. I'm talking about real, real morality, integrity. This was actually one of the points I raised during that conversation that we had in Gainesville before or after it was interrupted. I brought out, I suggested that one difference between the West and us, ourselves, the non-Westerners, in our conception of literature, in our conception of art, is this component of morality. And I suggested from the Igbo cosmology, the Igbo theology, my own native tradition, that it is not accidental that the earth goddess, Earth, is not only the goddess of morality, but she is also the goddess of art. This conjunction is not accidental. Art is fundamentally, is founded in, morality. That art which is important, which is meaningful, cannot be indifferent to moral issues, to serious issues, to political issues, to social concerns. Some years ago at a conference in Stockholm, a Swedish journalist from a very famous family, his father was one of the world's great anthropologists or sociologists and his mother was a member of the cabinet, said, you African authors are very lucky. At least your governments care enough to put you in prison. Here in this country, no matter what you say, nobody pays any attention. So we said to him, we are sorry, you know, we are sorry for you. We sympathized. But really, if you look at it, there's a very important point there. I think, Michael, you referred to that.

Artists have themselves played a role in downgrading their profession. The conflict between the poet and the emperor is fundamental. There is no way you can see it in any other way. And where you have the poet not bothering about, when you have the emperor not bothering about the poet, you can be sure that something is wrong. Because they should. I was saying this the other day in Pittsburgh, I can't see a novelist in Britain for instance writing a novel that will make Mrs. Thatcher want to lock him or her up. I don't see a novelist in this country writing a novel that will make Reagan have sleepless nights. And this in itself says something about the quality of the novels being written. The artist has been persuaded that he doesn't have a responsibility in that direction and the emperor is very happy. You know, you talk about other things, important things, you know, the life of the society, the quality of the civilization, you know, all kinds of things, but nothing that will make the emperor want to sit up and ask where is that man? Go and get him. And as long as that happens, the artist is failing in some way, in my view. With all due respect, with all due respect to the talent and the expertise and the excellence that have been displayed, this fundamental conflict between art and authority is one way in which an artist can judge whether he is doing, he/she is doing, their proper job. And this is the significance of Baldwin, you know. He stood quite clearly and quite firmly on the side of the artist using his talent to call things by their name, including saying that the emperor has no clothes. And if you say this, you're not going to be very popular with the emperor, but you will be doing your work.

TERRY: I think we have time for questions.

THELWELL: In this particular case, the emperor not only has no clothes, he deaf, dumb, and blind, as El Haji Malik used to say.

TERRY: If you'd like to join in the conversation by questions or comments, please feel free to do so and may I ask if you would use the microphone right here in the center, please.

AUDIENCE: Mr. Achebe has told us how he met James Baldwin and when. Could each of you tell us about your first meeting with him?

THELWELL: I was a student at Howard University involved with a number of other students on that campus. Howard University, for those of you who don't know, is a Black school in Washington, D.C. At the time of the sit-in movement, we determined, some of us, that being in the nation's capital, we had a particular historical responsibility, the White House and the Capitol being easily available. So we organized students to go and make the emperor a little unhappy. And an associate of ours who was White came over and said, does the name James Baldwin mean anything to you? And I said, yeah, he's a writer, he's some kind of writer. What have you read by him? Nothing. He said, listen, he is the most extraordinary little Black man from Harlem you will ever meet and he gave about a five minute description of Jimmy which proved to be quite accurate. One of the things he said was, he's just absolutely one of the most brilliant and luminous intelligences he ever saw, but his personal life is always in a state of chaos. And that he skates on the very brink of disaster all the time emotionally and that proved to be true in the length of time I knew him, this was 1960. He says, he's giving a talk in Georgetown and he particularly asked that some of the movement kids, which is how we were referred to then, be invited. So a group of us left Howard University and went over into Georgetown, which was pretty much alien territory. And found this big mansion, the home of a wealthy former socialist, walked in a little bit late, a room which may have been half the size of this one, but about as many people, actually there were probably more than is in this room right now, in a huge circle against the walls. And in the center, this slim dynamic little figure. James Baldwin, as I've written somewhere, surrounded by White America.

And the door opens and about ten of us Black young people walk in and everything comes to a stop and Jimmy looks up towards the door, sees us and with a kind of spontaneous delight and joy, his whole face just erupted into a smile and any of you who've seen Jimmy smile know that that was one of the other geniuses he had. Ain't nobody could smile like him. And the whole face was transfigured and he said, "Hi, I'm Jimmy Baldwin and I'm so happy that you came." And we walked in and he gave a discourse on the problem of race and I quite literally had never heard anything like it. He was so eloquent, so precise in his use of language and so incisive in his thought that, you know, many people will have seen him on tape, many people will have heard him, people have even heard him lecture personally. But at this time he was thirty-five years old, at the very height of his power and his engagement, the years hadn't taken a toll yet. And the country was about to, was locked in conflict which was about to explode, and everybody could sense that. I mean it was an electric time in the country. And to walk into this group of White folk, in 1960, we'd just started to sit-in and do everything else that was going to shake and move this country and hear Baldwin talking about this. And everyone of the shibboleths, every one of the prejudices, every one of the biases, every one of the attitudes that had been so unconsciously, uncritically accepted by White America, even by White American scholarship. All the nonsense about race that they used to believe, he just systematically and skillfully demolished, so that you kind of had to testify. *"Tell it Brother, mm-hm, right on!"* And we just start to getting badder as we listened. Then he went to the questions and White America was bemused. And there was a long pause before the first question, somebody raised their hand, "Were you saying . . ." and then tried to redefine the questions. And he dropped on them worse this time and you could see that, and these were well-intentioned people, now, these were progressives, so they called themselves. But they never had thought about these questions in quite that way. And they kept putting forward the questions, seeking for clarification, hoping maybe that he would back down, that he would retract. And what he had done, essentially, in a way that was indisputable, was place the responsibility for a racial problem. First of all he says, it's not a Negro problem. Let's not call it a Negro problem anymore. This is an American problem. He said, in point of fact, you have a White folks problem. Since I, he says, know that I have never been a nigger, nor my mother, nor my brother. White America has to start thinking about why he needed, why it needed to create that. What is it in the White American consciousness that needed this myth? Why did it create it, or why have they constructed themselves? And they never had the responsibility of facing them before. And the ground moved, it really did. And the questions became more and more belligerent and more and more futile, because Jimmy had an answer, and I don't mean a studied political answer, Jimmy answered with the remorseless logic of truth. And at the end, you know, you could see people shaking their heads as though they were punch-drunk, numb, trying to refigure the universe, because he had revolutionized it.

I can't imagine better circumstances to be introduced to a person. We left the place James Baldwin fans. Next day we went to campus, everybody was reading his book. And I'll say one more thing. He came onto the campus to discuss the responsibility of the Black writer and about six o'clock one morning he made a compact with us and again it was the movement kids, as we were referred to. And we'd been up all night talking. Lots of people had come in. Poitier had come in to listen, Sidney Poitier, dressed in an overcoat and dark glasses and smuggled himself into the auditorium incognito, you know. I was sitting up in this apartment, a little bit drunk and very very excited, and he says, I, Jimmy Baldwin, as a Black writer have a certain responsibility to you, my young brothers and sisters, and to my mother and to my father and to generations before, I have that responsibility. I didn't seek it, and you didn't give it to me, but there we are. He always would say, but there we are, you know. He says, and I can promise you and we can make a compact here today that if you never accept the reductive and racist and pejorative definitions that this republic has prepared for you, and I know they have them, if you never accept those, I, Jimmy Baldwin, will never betray you. I took it seriously. I know everybody in that room took it seriously and it's clear from the example of his work, from the example of his life, that he certainly took it seriously and honored it.

McCLAURIN-ALLEN: I don't think my contact was quite as dramatic as Mike's. I had the privilege of meeting Baldwin when he came here in 1984. Prior to that I had read his works. But one of the wonderful things is that he had the most extraordinary capacity for making one feel as if you had known him for much longer. And so I was privileged to meet him at that time and during the succeeding times that he was here until his death.

WIDEMAN: Mahar Auditorium, I guess it had to be 1984. I was here to give a talk and I arrived early and someone picked me up and said, oh, would you like to, you have an hour or two before your talk, would you like to go hear Jimmy Baldwin? Yes, I would love to go hear Jimmy Baldwin. I would come for that reason and let me skip my talk, and etc., etc. 'cause I'd only known him from a distance. I'd known him in a way as one writer knows another. I knew him in terms of his language. To read a word like "conundrum," it was almost as if he had this business that he was in and he could go out and like a, sort of like a developer he'd go out and acquire all this language and make a claim to it that nobody could deny and then bring it home. You know, not, we could buy little plots of it and it was ours and he reminded us how this language was something that we were heir to and that we could not only buy these plots, but then we could make homes on them. We could turn it and use it. So that's the way I knew him, from a distance, you know, his power and force and the kind of magical proprietor of the language. So it was extremely exciting for me.

But I want to turn the story a little bit so it can be used in some ways, because it wasn't a very dramatic reading, meeting. Mr. Baldwin, my name is John Wideman, how are you? I really enjoyed your talk. But the talk was the point. He was discussing the civil rights movement, and whatever he had to say, which was an awful lot, in a very discursive kind of free-flowing improvisational Afro-American form. But when somebody on stage says, "And then Malcolm said to Martin," it gets my attention. But so I'd listened to that, then I'd listened to his students in Mahar Auditorium respond to this lecture and that was very fascinating also, because it became clear that people had come to hear Baldwin, but they had brought a lot of baggage with them. And I saw sort of in embryo, or in miniature in that audience, what happened to Baldwin's talk and books when they were introduced to the larger society. People didn't hear them. They kind of wrote letters to one another. This person talked to that person about what they thought Baldwin said. This audience addressed members of the same audience about things that they thought Baldwin had said. And he was the missing turn. Often what he said got lost. And that was so frustrating, so difficult. But I met him, we shook hands, and then my experience was very much like Irma's. I had a chance one or two times after that with my family to sit down and have a meal and it was wonderful.

THELWELL: I want to respond to something. I want to take an extraordinary risk, something I wouldn't do easily, to disagree a little bit with my esteemed brother here. Because, not really to disagree, to explain it, because what he says is true, up to a certain point. But one has to distinguish between the principalities, the apparatchiks and the institutions of culture, and the people. Because I did have the opportunity and the privilege of travelling around with Jimmy on occasion when he'd go to speak and places like that, or just being in a bar having a drink or something. And it wasn't the kind of face you could mistake, you know, people would look and then they would say, yeah, yes, that's him, I mean, they'd walk up in awe. I mean, is that really James Baldwin? And on these occasions, we didn't get into a closed contextual discussion of the books, but people, Black and White, came up and said with fervor, and with passion in their voice, and sometimes they would go into detail, that in point of fact, the works had moved them, that the works had changed their lives, that the works had redefined their perceptions of the country. And the strangest and most improbable people would go out of their way to come up and testify in that way. And you could see in their faces, now what they actually got out of those works we can't be sure, but you could see in their faces that those works had been effective. And everywhere that I went with him that happened, and happened in large numbers. And there were always people of a certain generation, people in their forties or fifties, I don't know if the younger generation has the same exposure, but people who lived through the 50s and the 60s and the early 70s, and in enough numbers to suggest that the work has in fact been very, very consequential, that there is a generation of Americans who understand the world, certainly at least understand this country and the question of racism, largely in terms given to them by James Baldwin. I think that is true.

AUDIENCE: I would like the writers to say something about the relationship between music and the written word. If we look at Ralph Ellison, for example, who is a musician, Charles Fuller, we look at August Wilson, James Baldwin, they all talk about the effect music has had upon their language, or their writing. And I want to know first of all, has music affected your writing? And specifically how music impacts on the written word.

McCLAURIN-ALLEN: All I can say is, this morning when I got up, I turned on Aretha to get myself ready and I don't know if I can articulate as eloquently, you know, as Ralph Ellison has about the interrelationships, because I'm not a musician, but clearly the language, the rhythm, the kinds of things that inform my poetry are directly related to the same kinds of rhythms and patterns that derive from music. Again, perhaps not in a formal kind of sense, but there's no doubt about it in my mind at all, that there are multiple forms of musical discourse that are woven into the lives and the language of Black people, and that's where I take my work from, my imagery, the language that I use. So I'm not sure if that's a direct answer, but, that's where I'll start.

THELWELL: It's the whole cultural approach, my brother. In Africa, the distance between music, poetry, language and song is very very close. In the Afro-American tradition, what we see is the precise conceptual process that constitutes improvisational jazz and the way one has recourse to a tradition and yet themes and motifs alter it and interweave it. Precisely this same process occurs in the Afro-American song sermon, exactly the same process. There is not a great, you mentioned Ellison, you mentioned Baldwin, there is not a great Afro-American writer who isn't very close to that tradition and it doesn't take a hell of a lot to look into it. I mean, if critics would, you know, abandon this jargon which so disfigures their prose, I mean this deconstruction bullshit, and start going back to the business of criticism, you could display in Baldwin's prose, and some of his fiction also, that there is precisely the same organizational conceptual framework that a good preacher employs with the oral tradition, that a good jazz musician does with the jazz tradition, to a whole body of images and metaphors, which is what I tried to suggest when I said that his work was a distillation of Black culture. And that the process is the same . . . is very similar in all those forms, and that's why they resemble each other so closely; and you can see it if you look.

ACHEBE: Yes, well I think, I, you know, I can't talk about music in a technical sense, in the sense in which the last speaker is using it, I think there's no question at all that poetry, music, and good prose do in fact, share this concern for a certain movement, certain repetitions, a certain curve, and the best writers, writers like Baldwin, are very much concerned with this, with euphony and with rhythm. A word is placed there and it is the right word in every sense. It's not just there because it's the first one that comes to hand. And so music in that sense, yes, there's a very close relationship. And furthermore if you are dealing with other languages, like my own Igbo language, which is very much a tonal language you'll find that, a tonal language is actually like singing. In these languages, the relationship to music is very very close indeed. And so if you wrote a certain word, like AKWA for instance, just seeing it, seeing the letters, wouldn't tell you what the word was. You have to sing it in order to get the meaning, the particular meaning you want. And different tones: whether it is low-high, high-low, low-low, etc., would determine the meaning. The same four letters but four different words according to the tone patterns you adopt. It's really musical, you know, dealing with musical scores; and so language and music are very very close indeed.

THELWELL: My brother, were you here this morning? You heard John Wideman's reading. Then it's a good example of what I was talking about. You know, John Wideman is doing, he's always doing good writing, but he's doing some of the best writing he has ever done recently. I mean, he writes his behind off. And if you heard, if you heard that reading this morning, you can see what I meant about the improvisational structure and the rhythms and the cadences and repetitions of the best jazz music, because John is exploring the possibilities of black vernacular speech in literature in a way that nobody else is doing with the same kind of success. Afro-American vernacular speech, and if you look at that, how that composition was put together, that prose poem he read this morning is exactly what I was talking about in a song sermon and in jazz and that was a quality that Jimmy pioneered, almost, and instructed us all in. But that's a good example of what I was talking about.

AUDIENCE: I'll just make a comment and maybe we can talk about it later or on other occasions. I think the problem of the moral, the moral work of the writer, is even more serious and conditions are even worse than you've described. I think one reason for this was hinted at, hinted at in the comment John made about the fate of Baldwin's writing, as it was disseminated in American discourse. I think of the great moral tradition of British and American novel writing, think of the 19th century, George Eliot, Conrad,

Hardy, Lawrence, Virginia Woolf, Joyce. Something's changed. Certainly those writers did not abandon the sense of themselves as the conscience of their race, but something's changed in the cultural conditions that affect all writers. It's certainly changed in America and in complex ways in Europe also. And if it hasn't changed in Africa in the same way, or in China, then there may be some hope for the moral position of a writer in America, but it seems to me that the conditions have, in a sense, made the emperor so diffuse that the problem of the writer is even deeper than we've acknowledged.

TERRY: That profound comment could be the occasion for another conference. I thank you very much for being with us for this conference. It's been very meaningful for us and we've been gratified by your presence and your attention.

NOTES ON CONTRIBUTORS

CHINUA ACHEBE is the author of five novels—*Things Fall Apart, No Longer at Ease, Arrow of God, Man of the People, Anthills of the Savannah*—and several volumes of verse, short stories, criticism, children's stories. He has received numerous honors and awards from different parts of the world, including eleven honorary doctorates from universities in Britain, U.S.A., Canada, and Nigeria.

From 1972 to 1976 he taught at the University of Massachusetts at Amherst as Professor of English and at the University of Connecticut, Storrs, as a University Professor of English. In 1981 he took early retirement from the University of Nigeria, Nsukka, with which he had been associated since 1967. He was made Emeritus Professor in 1985. In 1987-88 he was a Fulbright Professor at the University of Massachusetts at Amherst in the W.E.B. DuBois Department of Afro-American Studies.

KETU KATRAK is an Assistant Professor in the English Department of the University of Massachusetts at Amherst and is at present a Fellow of the Bunting Institute at Radcliffe College. She was educated at Bombay University and Bryn Mawr, where she received her doctorate, and has taught at Howard University. The author of *Wole Soyinka and Modern Tragedy: A Study of Dramatic Theory and Practice* and co-editor with James Gibbs and Henry Louis Gates of a bibliography on Soyinka, she is at work on a book on Third World women writers.

IRMA McCLAURIN-ALLEN was born in Chicago, Illinois, and attended Grinnell College in Iowa, receiving a B.A. in American Studies. In 1976 she completed the M.F.A. in English at the University of Massachusetts, where she works as an Assistant Dean while pursuing a Ph.D. in Anthropology. Her latest book of poetry is *Pearl's Song* (Lotus Press, 1988). She resides in Amherst, Massachusetts with her family and a host of supportive friends. At present, she is completing *Incongruities: A Biography of Leanita McClain*.

ANDREW SALKEY is a Jamaican novelist and poet, author of numerous volumes, and Professor of Writing at Hampshire College, Amherst, Massachusetts.

ESTHER TERRY is Associate Director of the Institute for Advanced Study in the Humanities and Chair, W.E.B. DuBois Department of Afro-American Studies at the University of Massachusetts at Amherst. She was educated at Bennett College, the University of North Carolina, and the University of Massachusetts, where she earned her doctorate in English with a dissertation on Richard Wright.

MICHAEL THELWELL is a Jamaican writer and Professor of Afro-American Studies at the University of Massachusetts, in the department of which he was the first Chair, from 1969 to 1975. He was educated in Jamaica, at Howard University (B.A., 1964) and at the University of Massachusetts (M.F.A., 1969). His publications include *The Harder They Come* (Grove, 1980) and *Pleasures, Duties and Conflicts: Essays in Struggle* (Massachusetts, 1987). He was Director of the Washington Office of S.N.C.C. and then the Mississippi Freedom Democratic Party from 1963 to 1965.

JOHN EDGAR WIDEMAN joined the English Faculty of the University of Massachusetts at Amherst in 1986, where he teaches creative writing and Afro-American literature. Previously, he had been a professor of English at the University of Wyoming, Laramie.

Born in Washington, D.C. in 1941 he grew up in Pittsburgh. Wideman graduated from the University of Pennsylvanis with a B.A. in English in 1963. He was Captain of the basketball team and elected to the Philadelphia Big Five Basketball Hall of Fame. He was one of two Black Americans to receive Rhodes scholarships in 1963—the first since Alain Locke in 1907.

As a Rhodes scholar Wideman spent three years in England, receiving a B.Phil. degree from Oxford in 1966. He subsequently spent a year at the University of Iowa Writers Workshop.

Wideman's widely-praised books include the novels *A Glance Away,* 1967, *Hurry Home,* 1969, and *The Lynchers,* 1973. A collection of short stories, *Damballah,* and the novel *Hiding Place* appeared in 1981, *Sent For You Yesterday* in 1983. The non-fiction *Brothers and Keepers* was published in 1984. *Damballah, Hiding Place,* and *Sent For You Yesterday* were re-issued by Avon in 1984 as *The Homewood Trilogy.* The novel *Reuben* was published in 1987 (Holt).

OTHER IASH PUBLICATIONS ALSO AVAILABLE:

Occasional Papers I
Jules Chametzky, "Aims, Work, Relevancy of Centers of Advanced Study"
Julius Lester, "Humanity and the Humanities"
R.C. Lewontin, "Science as a Social Weapon"

Occasional Papers II
Leonard Charles Dickinson, "A Quest for Connection: A Confessional Reflection on the Insufficiency of Hard Science to Map onto Hard Life"
Jean Bethke Elshtain, "From Machiavelli to Mutual Assure Destruction: Reflections on War and Political Discourse"
Dennis Porter, "Response to Jean Bethke Elshtain"

Occasional Papers III
Richard O'Brien, "Values in the University"
Ervin Staub, "The Ideal University in the Real World"

Writers Speak: Writers on Writers and Social Responsibility
Jay Neugeborn, "Making Stories"
Shulamith Oppenheim, "Educating the Imagination"
Michael Thelwell, "As Sounding Brass or a Tinkling Cymbal: Modernist Fallacies and the Responsibility of the Black Writer"

Writers Speak: America and the Ethnic Experience
Alan Lelchuk, "The End of the Jewish Writer?"
Jerre Mangione, "Remembrances and Impressions of an Ethnic at Large"
John Edgar Wideman, "Black Fiction and Black Speech"